commune

DESIGNED IN CALIFORNIA

Roman Alonso   Steven Johanknecht   Pamela Shamshiri   Ramin Shamshiri

with contributions by

Lisa Eisner
Mallery Roberts Morgan
Mayer Rus
Matt Tyrnauer

ABRAMS, NEW YORK

For those of us who live in the Wild West, freedom is the word. There's so much space, literally and figuratively. It's the land of opportunity. A place where history is of little consequence. A place for self-invention. We can only imagine what it must have been like for those first adventurous souls who crossed the Mississippi and headed toward the Pacific. There are still moments today, driving through central California, or even the canyons in Malibu, when we can almost experience what they saw when they arrived, particularly at twilight, that magical hour before sundown. There's nothing like it in the whole wide world. After crossing the Rockies, and then the Arizona and Nevada deserts, it must have seemed like paradise. It still does. The weather alone is half of it. The other half is that intangible thing you feel in the air here, that freedom.

In Western films, when the new guy in town walked through the doors of the saloon the color of his hat was the window into his character: black = bad, white = good. Now we don't even wear hats. Out here the new guy in town is whoever he wants to be. No rules apply. In New York, people will try their best to figure you out. They'll ask questions to pull out of you useless information like where you went to school, as if it matters. In Los Angeles, nobody asks about your past; they are too afraid they will be asked the same question. You are only as great as the last film you made, or the last book you wrote, or the last yoga class you taught. Judgment is fleeting, memories short. For those who are dabblers or interested in many things, for those who refuse to conform or have a hard time figuring out what to put on that line that says "occupation," LA has always been the place.

California's cultural contributions are huge, particularly in modern living. Contributions that the world is only now starting to fully embrace. After decades of perceiving Los Angeles as a cultural void, now everyone wants a piece of the "California lifestyle." Undoubtedly that yearning for "the life" starts with the weather and nature and light. It's simple: Here, you just want to be outside; you want to lay back, you just want to relax. The California lifestyle is a house that has no style; or better yet, is in any style; or is of a multitude of styles. It's whatever you want it to be as long as it lets the sunshine in and invites you to hang out.

Back when California was Nueva California it was all Spanish ranch houses. Designed for work, they were right for the landscape. When the Europeans landed and started making money, they brought with them Gothic and Tudor and Renaissance styles with little regard for the resulting mash-ups—anything went—and for better or worse, it continues. But it's thanks to the modernists that we are on the architecture world map today. Their experiments in living changed everything. All bets were off, one could live on very little, and there was reason to let the world in—it was beautiful. Add to that the California arts and crafts movement, and the artisans and tradition of great craftsmanship that came with it, and it all adds up to something that's free and easy and has a hand to it.

This freedom from the past and disregard for the rules has made California a mecca for creative types and for those who can make things. Because of the beauty of the place and wealth of available resources you are constantly inspired and feel free to try things out, to exercise your creative urges. As we write this, an exodus is taking place, moving west. Artists, designers, filmmakers, writers—hello LA! There are few places on earth where you are as connected and yet as free of conventions as you are here. Because there's no pulse of fashion or style to put your finger on. Because you have all the physical and emotional space you want. Because all is forgiven. You can try it all out, and possibly fail. For the past ten years Los Angeles has provided the freedom and inspiration to break all the rules. The room to design and create literally whatever we want. Permission to be us... to be Commune.

In New York you must look up that ladder and climb it to achieve success. In California all you have to do is look out into the horizon and anything is possible.

commune

5

inside commune

Photographs and text by Lisa Eisner

I remember when Commune was just a seed of an idea, not even a sprout yet—just four very imaginative people from different stomping grounds figuring out how to bring their design sense into a shared orbit. Living in Los Angeles was a very important part of the adventure. They saw LA as a place for defining lifestyles. California has always been a place for alternative living, collectives, craftsmanship, loving the land, free thinking, earth mamas and papas, and definitely a no-rules "Let's just do what we think looks right" attitude. There were no models, really, except of course the very king and queen of design: the Eameses. It was Charles Eames who once said: "Eventually everything connects—people, ideas, objects...The quality of the connections is the key to quality per se. I don't believe in this 'gifted few' concept, just in people doing things they are really interested in doing. They have a way of getting good at whatever it is."

Charles' words remind me of Commune. The founders all love design, and each brought something different to the collective. Of the four partners, one is a professor of store design; one a crackerjack in fashion and book publishing; and the other two are visionaries in production design for movies and commercials. Four people trusting each other and agreeing and disagreeing a lot; having the perfect collaboration and contributing to each other's work, yet each with strong ideas and each bringing gifts from different areas and somehow coming together in the same direction; all believing that good design can improve the quality of life.

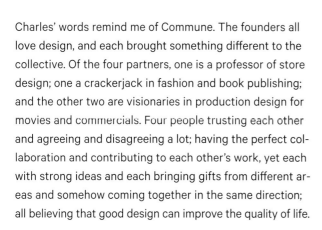

I have been through the doors of Commune more times than I can count. It's always buzzing, there's always an inspiration board going up, and there's always lots of textiles, furniture, blueprints, models, samples everywhere, and lots and lots of other things to look at. The studio is a think tank of young graphic designers, architects, and artists, all of whom love design, want to make things and have fun with it, and not take themselves too seriously. They work in teams and are encouraged to cross over in practice, so a graphic designer might work on an interior design project, or an architect, because of the way he or she draws, may be included in a team working on graphics. Whether a shampoo bottle or a couch, from a trailer to an estate, Commune doesn't limit itself. There's no model for a group like Commune. They are making it up as they go. If it can be designed, they'll do it. There is an innocence to their design process, a feeling that anything is possible.

As far as style goes, Commune is very California, and that sensibility is something they are still helping to define. It's bohemian but clean, and it's not afraid of color or pattern or texture. Their work never seems egotistical. It's organic. They want to be part of the environment and never take it over. It's always soulful, honest, a little hippie, and they love, love, love wood. If they have a signature, I would say it's their use of natural finishes and their emphasis on the handcrafted. They seek out artisans and bring them into every project, and in the process they have launched many careers. Like all good communes, they don't want to be the ones who take credit for everything. Commune has a unique synergy, playful yet practical and functional. They work with artists and craftspeople who make beautiful things, and bring them into their extended family and show the world what it means to truly collaborate. They show the world what the word "community" really means.

From the start, Commune has been innovative, always morphing, evolving, ripening. Who knows what beautiful thing they will grow into? I can't wait to see.

A HUNTING LODGE IN OJAI

PHOTOGRAPHS BY FRANÇOIS HALARD   TEXT BY RAMIN SHAMSHIRI

Upon entering the driveway of the Libbey House, you can't help but exhale as the northern gable of its large pitched roof comes into view. A feeling of calm transports you back to the early Californian countryside. Built in 1908, the house was architects Myron Hunt and Elmer Grey's first Craftsman-style project. Their Pasadena office was known for its work on the Beverly Hills Hotel, Occidental College, Pomona College, the Huntington Library, the Ambassador Hotel, and the Rose Bowl. By most accounts, it was primarily Hunt who worked on this house, which was conceived as the winter home of Edward Libbey, arguably Ojai's greatest patron. Libbey worked with several notable architects—among them, Wallace Neff (Ojai Valley Inn and Libbey Ranch), Mead and Requa (Libbey Park, Ojai Arcade, and Post Office), and George Washington Smith (various residences in the Arbolada)—to create many of the iconic structures of modern Ojai.

Libbey originally purchased more than three hundred acres of land, which he eventually developed into a neighborhood known as the Arbolada. He chose his homesite for what he felt were the best views in the Ojai Valley, and he worked closely with Hunt to create a home that integrated well with the striking landscape.

When we first saw it, the house was decorated in furnishings appropriate to the arts and crafts era. We wanted to create something more comfortable and amenable to entertaining and spending time with immediate and extended family, so we worked with furniture that, while not necessarily from the era, was inspired by it: pieces handcrafted from materials that aged gracefully by designers such as George Nakashima, Alma Allen, Michael Wilson, and Adam Kurtzman, among others. The house had such great bones and history that we felt it would be easy to make it look good. Our challenge was to create a modern environment that worked for how we live today and yet resonated with this beautiful historic setting.

<< The garden on the street side of the house is a classic early-twentieth-century California garden with its fusion of primitive and picturesque naturalism.

< A portrait of an Indian chief attributed to early California painter Walter Ufer hangs on a wood-paneled wall in the great room.

The great room has the look of an old lodge. Ojai legend has it that the Chumash stenciling on the beams and front door was done by an Indian chief in gratitude to Mr. Libbey, who had an excellent relationship with the local tribes. Our aim was to create one large seating area around the stone hearth and to light the room in a way that feels appropriate to its roots. Because of the large size, nearly every piece of furniture was custom-made. The coffee table is cast bronze and walnut by Alma Allen. The armchair in the foreground is by Wikkelsø.

The primary entrance to the house is on the east side, facing the backyard. Through an exceptionally wide Dutch door, you enter the sunroom, which was originally the rear deck of the house, but was converted to a sunroom with accordion windows sometime in the 1980s. We decided to keep it as a sunroom, and today it's a sitting area with rattan furniture by Paul Frankl. Toward the back of the room, we built out a vintage semicircular bar with a copper counter and semicircular drawers. It is surrounded by four large wooden stools by Andrée Putman and is a great gathering spot for sunset cocktails before supper.

Outside the sunroom, a large deck overlooks the garden, with the arresting Topatopa Mountains as a backdrop. This deck was built on top of the garage when the previous deck was converted to the sunroom, but we replaced its composite decking with Mangaris wood to give it more of an old-world charm. We designed a massive outdoor sectional sofa as well as a large teak and cement-tile dining table, all with the intention of entertaining large groups. Libbey's intention was to build a retreat that felt like a Swiss hunting lodge: He fulfilled that wish, but with a California twist. This influence is most obvious in the open-plan living and dining rooms. All the interior walls are covered in old-growth redwood, and the massive stone fireplace is easily the heart of the home. We lightened the original Douglas fir floors to give the space a Swiss chalet look. A large goatskin rug lies in the living room with a custom coffee table by Alma Allen, and an arts and crafts–inspired sofa by Blackman Cruz sits on one side and a Nakashima-style bench sits on the other. Libbey was a generous supporter of the local Chumash Indians during his time in Ojai, and out of gratitude, a tribal leader painted the living- and dining-room ceilings with Chumash designs, which we left untouched. On the mantle is a gift passed down from the previous owners, an Irving Penn photograph of Igor Stravinsky, who stayed at the house when he conducted for the Ojai Music Festival. The custom chandelier we designed with Paul Ferrante hangs in the middle of the room, unifying it as one communal space.

The dining room hutch and buffet were designed by Myron Hunt. We restored them and placed them back in their original positions. The beloved plates are by Konstantin Kakanias. They are portraits of the family members—pets and all—as chickens! The wood dining table is by Michael Wilson. The chairs are Nakashima. The portrait was painted in 1922 by Italian artist Ferruccio Pizzanelli.

The adjoining dining room includes a wood carved table by Michael Wilson as well as a leaded glass chandelier by Adam Kurtzman. The chairs are Nakashima reproductions, and the two cabinets were original to the home, passed on from the previous owners. One of the cabinets was designed to display dishes, and we commissioned a set of plates featuring portraits of the family as chickens by the artist Konstantin Kakanias.

We painted the walls in the hallway to the bedrooms a rust color and wallpapered the ceilings to give it more warmth. The children's bedroom has the same wallpaper on the ceilings, but we painted the walls a light green with a hint of blue and added blue plaid carpet as well as a pair of early-1900 twin beds that we had lacquered in blue. The play area has vintage wallpaper with classic cars on it and contains a variety of vintage toys and books that we collected from local shops in Ojai.

All the windows in the sunroom bifold open. The room is filled with Frankl rattan pieces, vintage lights from Austria, a Moroccan rug, and a coffee table by Michael Wilson. The wood bar came from a deco movie theater and the stools are by Andrée Putman.

The master bedroom has a pitched ceiling and a balcony centered on the entire property. Much like those in the living and dining rooms, the walls in the bedroom are paneled in wood and most of the floor is covered in a Turkish Oushak. The furniture is a mix of styles and eras: The black lacquered bed is essentially a modern spin on early American furnishings, the Nakashima dresser sits beneath a landscape painting that hides the television, a Bruno Mathsson lounge chair joins a chandelier by Stephen White that the children consistently refer to as the "White Pumpkin."

Ultimately, I think we fulfilled our goal of creating a home respectful of its rich history, befitting the practical necessities of a modern family, and incorporating pieces from a variety of eras that embody today's California style.

< The master bedroom is lit by a large Stephen White lantern. The painting is an unknown early California oil that came with the house. We installed a television behind it. The dresser is original Nakashima.

The kids' room has a pair of Monterey-style twin beds. The play alcove was originally a screened-in porch. The wood-and-rattan bench is by Van Keppel-Green.

My sons, Paolo and Adello, and myself in our kitchen. The Monterey-style chairs and tiled table were among the few pieces that came with the house. The kitchen has an outdoor eating area in the courtyard beyond.

< The trellised arbor connects the main house to the larger of two guesthouses. The courtyard is below the master bedroom and adjacent to the pool cabana. The fountain came with the house and is made of early California pottery.

Since the house was one of the first residences in Ojai, it's on an incredible location on a promontory with a view of the Topatopa Mountains and beyond. It's true that you often get a "pink moment" at dusk in Ojai. The pool is tile and concrete and set into pea gravel. The stone walls mimic the original stone walls surrounding the property.

HIPPIE CAMPING

To be perfectly honest, the first time we visited the site our client Ace Hotels had proposed for its Palm Springs location, we had a hard time seeing it. It was originally a Howard Johnson's and more recently a Westward Ho and Denny's, but it had been abandoned and squatters and meth addicts had taken over—creepy doesn't begin to describe it. Still, the mountain views made you feel you were in the middle of nowhere, and infusing this motor-lodge relic in played-out Palm Springs with Ace's super-urban vibe was a challenge we couldn't pass up.

We loved Ace. Their hotel in Portland is an icon of brand purity. We are still fans of it. Ace shared our love of the California desert and our dislike of the banality of what had become the vernacular of the area. We knew the experience we would create together had to be democratic, purely American, and highly personal. So we dove into 1970s road movies and Westerns, M*A*S*H, and Native American culture. We looked at every hippie DIY thing we could get our hands on, from the *Shelter* book to the *Whole Earth Catalog*. We watched *Zabriskie Point* and *Billy Jack*. And slowly we started putting together the visual map for a modern/utopian/luxury/camping retreat.

Our first big move was placing all the parking on the outside perimeter of the six-acre site. The old parking areas became private patios for ground-floor guest rooms, communal fireplaces, landscaped picnic areas, and a massive events pavilion with retractable, twenty-foot, glass garage doors and an additional round swimming pool. We repurposed the old pool and made it bigger and better, adding a stargazing deck and an outdoor restaurant under the grove of date palms. We reclaimed the old lobby, the Denny's restaurant, and the old Amigo Room bar, and after digging through drywall, a million layers of bad paint, hideous carpet, and linoleum, we found the bones we needed for a resurrection.

The soul of the project came in the form of artisans, craftsmen, and vintage furniture. Together with Ace we made the decision to go fully Californian and not source anything outside of the state. We couldn't afford solar panels, but we were going to be as green as we could with the budget we had, and in the process we were going to support the locals. Local dealers sourced more than twelve hundred pieces of vintage furniture from the 1960s and 1970s, and we asked more than a dozen artists and artisans to contribute their talent to the design of the hotel. The commissions were highly collaborative in spirit, with much back and forth between Commune, Ace, and the artisan studios and workshops. We worked with Fresno ceramicist and legend Stan Bitters on communal fireplaces made of giant glazed ceramic tiles, and he ended up making concrete fire pits for the private patios, too. Joshua Tree sculptor Alma Allen turned a stool for every room and made his first cast-bronze pieces as door handles for the lobby. Los Angeles costume designer and jeweler Michael Schmidt made a curtain for the lobby out of Japanese bondage knots and eight miles of cotton rope. Artists Clare Crespo and Alice Spring fashioned a desert fantasy of a diorama for the lobby, including a pet coyote and a chorus of partridges wearing Mardi Gras beads. Free City made the bed covers, and our friends at Heath Ceramics made the Do Not Disturb signs out of kiln spacers. Stained glass windows by Steve Halterman ended up in the restaurant and stained glass–like vinyl collages by the artist Margo Victor went into the spa. At the end of the day, the hand of an artist, artisan, or craftsperson had touched every area of the hotel. The Ace Palm Springs truly represents a communal effort. It is the expression of a local community of designers, architects, artisans, artists, and craftspeople. It is a place built for all by all. It will always embody the philosophies that bind Commune to Ace.

PHOTOGRAPHS BY PAUL COSTELLO • TEXT BY ROMAN ALONSO

< The guest room patios were lined with concrete block in an open pattern. Inspiration for the desert pine gates came from 29 Palms Inn. Heath Ceramics made the Do Not Disturb signs out of glazed kiln spacers and rope.

Stan Bitters made concrete fireplaces for the patios. Cushions were covered in government-issue army tent fabric and vintage kilims.

We maintained the Howard Johnson's layout in most of the rooms because it worked; they knew what they were doing. Concrete floors were stripped bare. We added slatted wood walls and s-hooks so guests could "decorate" their rooms with tear sheets. Signature Ace bed bolsters were covered in hemp denim and the bed covers made of drop cloths were printed with a design by Free City. Alma Allen made bedside tables of steel and black walnut for record players. "Love Lights" designed by Robert Lewis, vintage kilims, and flannel djellabas rounded off the desert vibe.

We laid cork in the upstairs rooms and filled suites with vintage furniture sourced by local dealers in the desert area.

We placed the outdoor restaurant under a grove of date palms next to the pool.

For our way-finding signage, we drew inspiration from National Park signs.

> We unearthed the old Howard Johnson's restaurant beneath layers of horrible paint colors, carpet, and vinyl. We repurposed the old terrazzo floor and installed banquettes covered in saddle leather.

The original pool was doubled in size and a shaded area inspired by a Slim Aarons photograph was lined with hammocks.

We installed a desert diorama by the artists Alice Springs and Clare Crespo in the lobby featuring a pet coyote draped in Mardi Gras beads.

Costume and jewelry designer Michael Schmidt made a macramé curtain out of eight miles of cotton rope tied in Japanese-style bondage knots.

> Alma Allen's first cast-bronze sculptures were installed as the door handles to the lobby entrance.

The Schaffer House was an early John Lautner project built in 1949. Located in Glendale, a sleepy town adjacent to LA, the house was designed for the Schaffer family, who picnicked under the property's majestic California oaks and was inspired to live there permanently. The architecture was designed around the trees and oriented horizontally so that it nestles easily among them. Made largely of redwood and glass, the interior is composed of a series of small but open and interconnecting spaces. Wide, pivoting glass doors expand the main living area to the outdoors.

The property stayed in the Schaffer family, with one subsequent owner, until the late 1980s. In the following decades it was (fortuitously) bought and sold by a series of "Lautner-lovers." Most famously, it was the location for fashion designer Tom Ford's 2009 directorial film debut *A Single Man*. While Colin Firth was the film's lead actor, the house was unequivocally the star.

In January 2013 the Paris-based interiors publication *AD France* had the idea to photograph the house as a feature story. As their Los Angeles correspondent, it was up to me to find out about the property's current status. With a bit of sleuthing I soon discovered it had been sold that very week to a British commercials director, who had relocated to Los Angeles. Since he had not had time to move his belongings yet, the place was essentially empty. Our timing was perfect. For the *AD France* story, we asked Commune to furnish and decorate the house. The editor-in-chief of *AD France*, Marie Kalt, had been an early supporter of Commune. She featured one of their first residential projects as a cover story titled "The Keepers of the Cool." To a European eye, the Commune style is a chic, contemporary spin on California modern.

S O U S   L E   C H Ê N E

PHOTOGRAPHS BY JASON SCHMIDT   TEXT BY MALLERY ROBERTS MORGAN

Redwood-and-glass exterior patio with canvas-and-rope Salterini chairs from JF Chen, stone-and-mosaic table from The Window, and a 1960s ceramic sculpture by Robert Hardy from C Project.

> In the study, a Fabricius and Kastholm Grasshopper chaise lounge and African Lobi figures from C Project. Dombasli black-painted, single-arm, reproduction floor lamp from JF Chen. A Claro walnut hourglass stool by Alma Allen.

In the living room, a Frits Henningsen–style Danish sofa and matching armchairs, a Michael Wilson mulberry side table, and 1950s double-coned, red-painted, metal-and-brass floor lamp from JF Chen sit on top of a Commune rug for Decorative Carpets.

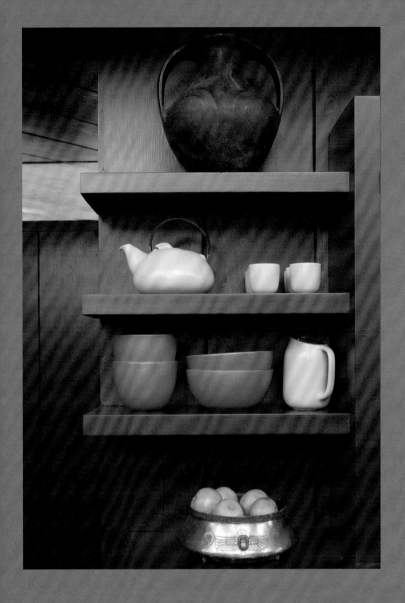

It took a week to install the house. First, everything had to be moved out and the house cleaned. The photographer Jason Schmidt was flown out to Los Angeles from New York. Sophie Pinet, features editor at *AD France*, came all the way from Paris.

Roman Alonso and Pam Shamshiri took the lead for Commune. They were like kids in a candy shop, decorating this beautiful house, which was so in tune with the Commune aesthetic, and "shopping" for all the things they love. As Roman said, "It was the perfect opportunity for us to be our own clients." Some of the dealers and shops that make the Los Angeles design community so unique and interesting participated by lending pieces: the great antiquarian Joel Chen of JF Chen, Gerard O'Brien of Reform Gallery, Heath Ceramics, Blackman Cruz, Galerie Half, and the florist Ariana Lambert of Lily Lodge. The Commune team brought their own stuff, too: pieces they make in collaboration with local artists and artisans and sell on the Commune website. Also, abstract paintings Steven Johanknecht paints in his studio at home; vintage books from Roman's personal collection; favorite vintage textiles and sheepskins from Pam's house.

Heath Ceramics dinnerware line the shelves in the kitchen.

> A custom dining set modeled after a Schindler design sits in the dining area. A 1950s Jacques Adnet leather, enameled-steel, and brass chair and Vicke Lindstrand ceramic gourd vase. All from JF Chen. The Coco de Mer on stands are from Galerie Half.

In the study, an English Regency–style, walnut-veneer settee from
C Project loaded up with vintage textiles and pillows sits across
from a 1960s George Nakashima, free-edge walnut coffee table
from JF Chen. The African Senufo masks are also from C Project.

"Being able to create something beautiful just for the sake of it; that's such a rare pleasure," said Roman. "Usually there are so many other considerations and people involved, this was like creating a vision of what this house would be if it were only for us."

The photo shoot, the images of which you see on these pages, lasted two days. When the shoot was finished, the decor was dismantled and disappeared piece-by-piece. Several months later, when I opened the magazine, there it was: Sous le Chêne. Commune meets Lautner under the California oaks—this time for everyone to see.

< A Charlotte Perriand double daybed from Galerie Half sits in the bedroom on a sheepskin rug from C Project. The desk chair is Arne Jacobsen, also from Galerie Half. On the bed a Noon Design, hand-dyed throw lies on top of an early American weaving.

The bathroom accessories are from Garde.

CERAMICS

Much like baking bread, making ceramics is sensual and primitive and mysterious. The earth, in the artist's hands, is thrown, coiled, built, shaped. As with dough, one gets intimate with the clay, and a bit of the soul naturally transfers into it. Glazing is a form of alchemy—you never know what you are going to get. The bowl you spent hours throwing and shaping may never make it out of the kiln, but when it does, it's always one of a kind; rarely will it do exactly what you had planned. The process is full of love and hope and trust and joy and disappointment. When you pick up a piece that survived the fire, you can't help but feel all of these things. We are addicted to that feeling. We've commissioned and worked with a number of ceramicists, from legends like Stan Bitters and establishments like Heath Ceramics to those who are in the process of putting California back at the forefront of this wonderful ancient art: Victoria Morris, Adam Silverman, Kevin Willis, and Simon and Nikolai Haas. — *Roman Alonso*

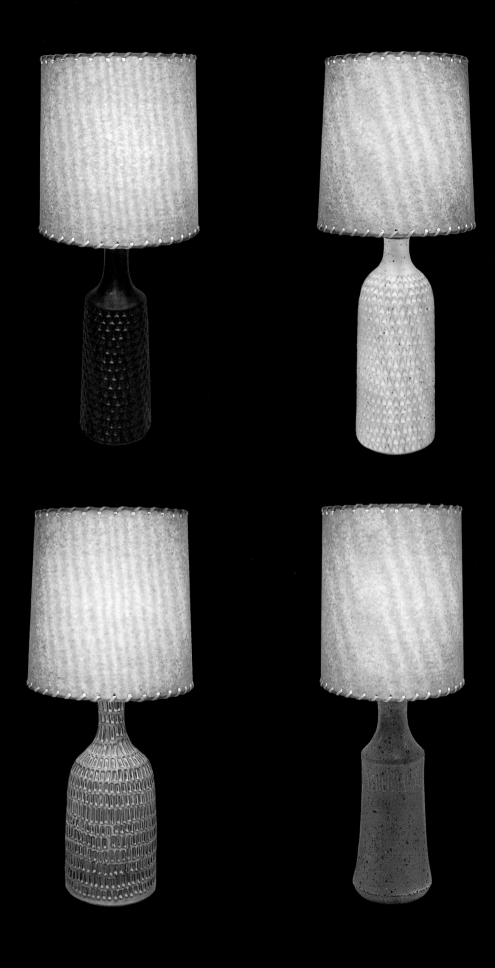

Bauhaus-inspired carved ceramic bowl, platter, and lamps by Victoria Morris.

We asked Heath Ceramics to leave our dinnerware "Nude" to show
the natural color of their signature clay.

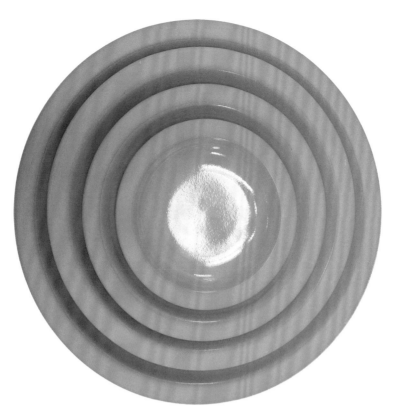

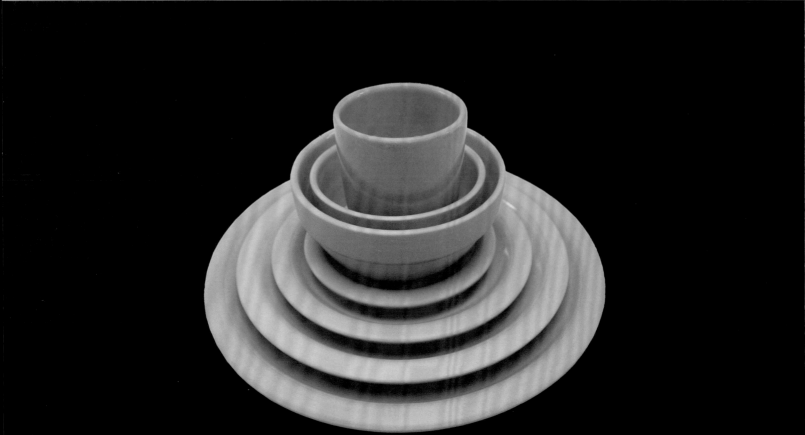

Limited edition canisters in collaboration with Heath Ceramics and Alma Allen. The glazes were inspired by the Bauhaus, and Alma hand turned the tops from walnut.

Buff & Now

Photographs by Richard Powers
Text by Pamela Shamshiri

Early mornings, driving across the ridge of the Hollywood Hills along sensual Mulholland Drive, you can't help but daydream of Los Angeles in the time of Case Study House experiments in the 1940s and 1950s and, later, of social upheaval and the radical designs of the 1960s. Here, residential living was reinvented forever.

As you pass several Schindler homes, a Neutra, Lautner's Rainbow house, and other architectural wonders, what stands out is the sprinkling of elegant Buff & Hensman post-and-beam houses of the 1960s. On the one hand, you sense that people are living off the grid here. On the other, Steve McQueen and Marlon Brando once lived nearby, so the area is downright swanky. It's easy to imagine twinkling lights, tweed blazers and dark turtlenecks, and cocktails in hand going on here. Donald Hensman choosing this as his place of residence and experimentation is easy to understand, too.

It's a windy descent from the ridge of the hills down into Nichols Canyon. Halfway down, the turn into the driveway is an extreme hairpin, both thrilling and worrisome. The gate opens and you descend toward an enclosed carport with an open, trellised room above.

The house is a quick walk down through a tunnel of overhead beams, cement pads, and black water fountains. It's a classic post and beam, but its barn wood cladding and layers of details give it a slickness that brings it into the present. Its pavilion style embodies indoor/outdoor California living at its best. It's a "machine for living," to paraphrase Le Corbusier, and in that spirit, we embraced technology; all can be controlled from your smartphone. You enter the house through a wide artisan-made, wood pivot door that opens into an elegant two-story volume. There, a Sergio Rodrigues console is our first nod to South American design. A floating cement and metal staircase leads upstairs to what we call the "light clouds." We collaborated on these lights with Robert Lewis, inspired by Bertoia sculptures. The entry space is open, relaxed, and streaming with light.

< View of the house toward the Ipe deck. The cabana houses the bathroom, the outdoor television, and the outdoor kitchen. The tile island is by Heath Ceramics. We added the cement bench inside the living room to balance the space and provide additional seating. The pot in the foreground is by noted California potter David Cressey.

The two-story entry foyer looking toward the front door. The console is by Sergio Rodrigues for Espasso. The overhead light is by Robert Lewis.

The living room has a Piero Lissoni couch in textured linen. The kilim pillows are by Commune. The wool pillows with leather trim are custom-made. The vintage bar cart under the stairs adds a bachelor-pad edge.

The vertical volume of the living room has exposed beams painted in a dark Benjamin Moore color and a soaring bronze, mirrored fireplace.

> Included in the collection of furnishings are a Contour chaise by Vladimir Kagan, a custom cocktail table by Alma Allen, and a floor lamp by Bottega Veneta. The black cowhide rug is by longtime collaborators and cohorts Grand Splendid.

The living room is also a vertical volume open to one side of the entry—an elegantly composed sculptural space. Sliding glass walls, open beams, wide overhangs, and a massive fireplace anchor the living room. We clad the fireplace in bronze mirror, which makes it soar. The rug is a deep black cowhide patchwork. A Piero Lissoni sofa, a Vladimir Kagan chaise, a South American bench, a Bottega Veneta floor lamp, and an Alma Allen table complete the collected experience. The pillows are more refined kilims in fabric inspired by menswear: cashmere, wool, tweed, leather, and shearling. Our primary focus for this space was keeping it warm. Architecturally, the datum line and beams do their job in bringing the space down to human scale. Texturally, the wood walls and fabrics kept this indoor/outdoor space warm, rooted, and down-to-earth.

On the other side of the wood wall that holds the staircase is the kitchen. We combined two rooms into one large kitchen with an enormous walnut island for both cooking and eating. The stainless steel kitchen is by Boffi, and it's outfitted with a bank of Miele appliances. What keeps the space balanced and warm are the handmade wall tiles and the carved tractor stools.

The industrial kitchen is outfitted with a Miele steam oven, coffee maker, and warming drawers. The stainless steel kitchen and plumbing fixtures are by Boffi, and the island countertops are custom made of oiled American black walnut. The tractor stools are by BassamFellows and the tile is by Heath Ceramics.

> The dining room features a picnic table and benches by Piet Hein Eek and a Franz West chain light. In the background is a Stan Bitters water wall that flows from the master bathroom above. The stairs in the far background lead to an office and an outdoor yoga pavilion above the garage.

The only dining room in the house is outside. With the push of a button, the infrared heaters turn on and heat-retaining shades roll down. A large retaining wall stands within feet of the back of the building, which we felt was problematic. We contacted architectural ceramicist Stan Bitters and asked him for a water wall that looked like a cross section of the earth. That is exactly what he delivered. Sitting at the Piet Hein Eek picnic benches and table, enveloped by the beauty of Dutch lacquer, you find yourself in this intimate outdoor dining room at the bottom of a two-story water wall. The Franz West chain light hanging over the table adds just a touch of Austrian brutalism.

The house has kept its secret, until now. Continuing outside toward the back deck and pool, you experience what we call the "180-degree turn" that Buff & Hensman are known for. This is the first time you realize the house is perfectly nestled into the crook of the canyon. Buff & Hensman had a gift for taking full advantage of a site: The house is private and seemingly surrounded by trees and yet, as you look to the side, the canyon unfolds before you. It's a jaw-dropping view—one of those rare deep-canyon vistas open to the sun.

The deck area is a party waiting to happen. The outdoor living room has a psychedelic brass fire bowl by Alma Allen. An Ipe cabana houses a kitchen, a full bathroom, and a hidden television.

< The deck at the back of the house holds the outdoor counterparts of everything in the house. It has a living room with a brass fire bowl by Alma Allen.

The outdoor kitchen has an island made of Heath Ceramic tiles and features Bertoia stools.

The cabana bathroom is made of Ipe decking and features Boffi plumbing fixtures.

The master bedroom and sitting area walls are covered in gray grass cloth by Astek Wallcovering. The green key rug is by The Rug Company. We found the vintage coffee table at Nickey Kehoe. The suede and wood armchair is vintage Swedish by Lief.

At the pool end, a small pool pavilion opens up, serving as the den and screening room. The deck above has the outdoor billiard table and feels like it's floating over the water. The last time we were at the house with Stan Bitters, he took a scan of the outdoor space and said, "Man, this isn't just a house, it's a happenin."

One of two guest bedrooms is upstairs with an en suite bathroom. The rest of the upstairs is the master suite, which is wallpapered in gray grass cloth. The house has no exposed drywall, a decision we made early on. A sitting area has a pair of wooden daybeds that are upholstered in cashmere. The green key rug is by The Rug Company. The bathroom is a skylit tile room. Again, the retaining wall was problematic in its proximity to this space. Once we clad it with the sculptural water wall, however, it started to rain and sing in there. Thanks to Stan, now it's one of the most memorable shower experiences in Los Angeles.

There is an intrinsic honesty to this house. The basic materials and spaces relate to a way of living. There are no gimmicks, just spatial grace and integrity. The humane proportions of the spaces and the comfortable materials make it warm and easy to live in. It's truly a house with a strong connection to its natural surroundings. You move from the inside to the outside seamlessly and unconsciously. It embodies the integration of a desired way of living and design that is unique to California.

Not many clients would be willing to embark on this kind of journey. Together, we took a nearly unrecognizable architectural gem and honored its past by restoring it spatially to its original design. We welcomed the house into the present by embracing technology and the way we live now. Our client pushed for this approach rather than for a strict restoration. He was right; in the end, this is far more interesting.

The master bathroom walls and ceiling are covered in a mix of tiles by Heath Ceramics.

> The bathtub and plumbing fixtures are by Boffi. Outside the window, running nearly the length of the room, is the Stan Bitters water wall. Quintessential Buff & Hensman skylights light the room.

< We slightly reconfigured the original pool. The water and sculpture wall above the hot tub is by Stan Bitters, and the pool tile is by Walk On tiles. We mixed a custom pool color to get the turquoise you see in this photo. The Ipe decking comes right to the edge of the pool. The gray walls in this photo have since been mirrored to reflect the canyon view. The pool pavilion serves as the den/screening room. It opens up completely and hovers over the pool. The terrace above it is the outdoor billiard room

This is the view from the pool toward the main house. The loungers and wood tables are by Carlos Motta for Espasso.

PHOTOGRAPHS BY SPENCER LOWELL & ILLUSTRATION BY ALIA PENNER
TEXT BY MATT TYRNAUER
FIRST APPEARING IN *T: NEW YORK TIMES STYLE MAGAZINE*. FEBRUARY 2014

ARTISTS UNITED

Before starting a new project Alex Calderwood, founder and creative director of Ace Hotels, always told himself a story. "That story was about the building, its heritage, the location, and, most important, who would inhabit it," says designer Roman Alonso, who, when Calderwood died unexpectedly in London at the age of forty-six, lost not only an important client, but an old and close friend. At the time of his death, Calderwood was working with Alonso and his LA-based firm, Commune, to put the finishing touches on the plans for the latest Ace, which opened in January 2014 in downtown Los Angeles.

Calderwood had been looking in other parts of the city for his sixth Ace project when he and his business partner, Kelly Sawdon, happened upon an all-but-abandoned building in Downtown's perennially down-at-the-heels theater district, whose main drag, Broadway, is lined with historic but faded movie palaces, long considered beyond resurrection. The building Calderwood bought had been the United Artists Theater, with an adjoining thirteen-story office tower, the one-time neo-Gothic headquarters of Texaco, which, when it was completed in 1927 was the tallest building in LA. "When Alex saw the United Artists building, and especially the theater, his mind began to reel," says Sawdon. "He said, 'You feel the soul in the place. I never walked into a building and was this overwhelmed.'"

The United Artists Theater's most recent owner/occupant had been the televangelist, Reverend Gene Scott, who embellished the building's façade with two massive neon signs, proclaiming JESUS SAVES. He broadcast from the 2000-seat auditorium, which was designed by C. Howard Crane in the dripping, gilded Spanish Gothic style. To either side of the proscenium are murals depicting the United Artists founders, Mary Pickford, Douglas Fairbanks and Charlie Chaplin, in heroic poses with Titian lighting and looming movie making equipment. Pickford is said to have instructed the architect to mimic the style of her favorite building: the cathedral in Segovia, Spain.

This pastiche of architectural and social history dazzled Calderwood, who set out to preserve it, build on it, and transform it into a thrumming hive of Hipsterdom. Last summer I stood with Calderwood and Alonso in the Commune design studio as we poured over thick binders of research on the history of United Artists, and examined pin-up boards lined with imagery that would inform the design of the hotel: stills from Pickford's silent movie oeuvre juxtaposed with shots from LA's 1980s punk scene; photos of the avant-garde Modernist architect Rudolph Schindler's 1922 house in West Hollywood next to images from Fritz Lang's Metropolis; Le Corbusier in his Cabanon next to rocker Richard Hell in a hotel room; Gloria Swanson next to singer Joan Jett.

"The narrative around the hotel goes like this," Calderwood explained: "Mary Pickford and Rudolph Schindler have an affair, and their love child turns out to be Exene Cervenka," the singer from the quintessential LA punk band, X. "The DNA of the place is very much the Flapper era, when Mary Pickford was the It Girl, and it seemed to us when we were pouring over the 1920s LA images and the early 1980s LA images, that there was a parallel. Both great, wild moments of revolutionary creativity, not to mention some experimentation and dangerous excess."

While the interior of the movie palace has been lovingly restored, the old office building had to be gutted in order to create 180 hotel rooms and public spaces. "When we stripped the old masonry away," says Alonso, "we realized that it was actually a brutalist cement frame structure—very Modern—in Gothic disguise. This brought to mind Schindler's house, with its sharp angles and poured concrete slab construction, and that became the inspiration for the rooms, where we left as much textured concrete exposed as possible."

The furnishing in the rooms is a fusion of spare, high Modernity and Hipster functionality: Platform beds covered in Pendleton blankets with Mondrian-inspired designs float over ironic "grandma gold" wall-to-wall carpeting. A Martin & Co. guitar sits in the corner, under a Noguchi lantern and next to a vintage Prouvé desk chair. The Ace color palate is dominated by muted earth tones—beige Homasote-lined walls, blond wood, gunmetal gray and brass fixtures--for a good reason, says Alonso: "Alex was colorblind. You would show him a red tile and he'd say, 'I love that shade of brown!'"

"What Alex was really interested in was people. Much more so than he was interested in design and architecture," says Alonso, who thinks that Calderwood would have been most pleased with public spaces in the hotel, which, beside the theater, include a rooftop café and pool inspired by Donald Judd's swimming pool at his compound in Marfa, Texas, and a lobby designed to house the legions of Ace-heads equipped with MacBook Airs who require ample "third place" hangouts to do their work and sip their Stumptown cappuccinos. "One of the most important things in terms of Alex's vision for this Ace is that he wanted to represent the spirit of LA from the time the original building was built until now," says Alonso. "It was really important for us to localize the project, to the point where almost everything in this building, from the lamps to art on the walls"—works by Mike Mills alluding to the LA news events of 1927, and murals by brothers Nikolai and Simon Haas depicting off-beat iconic LA imagery such as a topless Jean Harlow, Gloria Swanson doing a headstand, and palm trees shrouded in mist—"to the stained glass windows are made in LA."

Commune, which is the firm responsible for the Ace in Palm Springs, is also a made-in-LA operation, whose projects have always taken cues from the indigenous surroundings. Adds Alonso, "Anyone who knows the town will walk through this place and be able to feel the spirit of LA in the building."

<< The Ace Hotel in downtown LA is housed in a tower and theater complex that was originally designed by architects Walker & Eisen as the offices for Texaco Oil and built in 1927. The theater next door was designed by C. Howard Crane for Walker & Eisen and was commissioned by Mary Pickford as the flagship theater for United Artists, the film studio founded with Charlie Chaplin and Douglas Fairbanks, and Pickford.

The interior of the theater was inspired by one of Pickford's favorite buildings, the cathedral in Segovia, Spain. It was well maintained by Reverend Gene Scott, who owned it for thirty years starting in the 1970s. We restored the original plaster and changed the color scheme to something more in keeping with the Ace brand.

Local artist Emily Tracy created an altar in the ladies' lounge from a found bronze sculpture and abalone shells.

> The carpet is custom designed and inspired by a detail we found in a plaster ceiling on the mezzanine level in the theatre.

◄ THEATER
2 ▲ SEGOVIA HALL
WALKER ROOM
EISEN ROOM
3-13 ▲ GUEST ROOMS
R ▲ UPSTAIRS

We maintained the original floor in the tower's vestibule and opened it to the reception and restaurant. The ironwork on the doors is inspired by the original grill above them and was made locally by artisans. The lighting is custom-made by Atelier de Troupe. The Haas Brothers, Simon and Nikolai, used graphite to draw on all the plaster walls on the ground floor. In the vestibule they depicted California mountain ranges and palm trees; hieroglyphs representing LA's cultural history cover the walls of the restaurant and reception

All way-finding signage was designed using a Corbusier typeface stenciled on old movie script pages that were used as wallpaper.

> The reception desk was also designed by the Haas Brothers from original wood paneling reclaimed from the old offices upstairs and feature fifteen oil paintings of palm trees in smog. Behind the counter, local artist Tanya Aguiñiga covered the wall and hallway with wool from eight different kinds of sheep. A perforated metal bookcase that wraps around the whole space is used as a retail area. The light fixture is by Atelier de Troupe.

The style of the restaurant is Viennese coffee house meets LA.
The columns and coffee bar are clad in Commune Sitio Tiles
by Exquisite Surfaces. Tables are custom-made with unlacquered
brass tops. Chairs are Thonet. Light fixtures and millwork details
are inspired by Austrian secessionist designs.

We worked hard to maintain as many as possible of the original poured concrete ceilings and columns found throughout the building. On the rooftop lounge, we added stamped cement tiles inspired by Frank Lloyd Wright and bearing an abstracted Ace logo. The light fixture is designed by costume designer Michael Schmidt and made of vintage chain collected throughout a two-year period and vintage stage lights that were found in the theater next door. Across from the bar, the thirty-five-foot-long wall hanging by Tanya Aguiñiga is woven from hundreds of felt blankets.

The outdoor lounge on the roof has a coral tree planted in the middle. Four lanterns by ceramicist Adam Silverman hang from the tree by braided cables reminiscent of ropes found around trees in Shinto temples. The seating is traditional Mexican equipale furniture painted white. Tables and stools are by Alma Allen from pencil cedar. On the tables are clay Mayan-inspired candleholders by ceramicist Kevin Willis. The awnings are printed with a Navajo-inspired bandanna pattern by artist Alia Penner.

> The rooftop pool inspired by Frank Lloyd Wright's Ennis House. The loungers are from a Jean-Michel Frank design.

> A bar carved from the trunk of a cedar tree by Alma Allen.

We exposed the concrete ceilings in most of the guest rooms and installed Homasote on the walls for warmth. Most layouts were extremely challenging, so we decided on a ship's-cabin approach and made everything built-in. The millwork and furniture is all made of a stained medium-density fiberboard called Valchromat, with the exception of a toolbox stool, which was made by local architect Tony Morera and his son, Carlos, a Commune alumnus. The lighting is custom by Atelier de Troupe. The "Mondrianesque" blankets are by Pendleton. The lanterns are Akari lights by Isamu Noguchi.

The bathroom vanities are a custom design inspired by the balconies at the Bauhaus school in Dessau. We used steel casement windows as dividers and shower screens. Fixtures are from the .25 collection by Waterworks.

the japanese farmhouse on carnation street

In the Commune tradition, we had a detailed narrative for this house that we were convinced was absolutely true. The story began long ago with someone whom we believe was a Japanese engineer working in Los Angeles in the 1920s with Frank Lloyd Wright, Schindler, and Neutra, among others. He was working with early modernists but longed for traditional Japanese architecture. He finally had the opportunity to build his own house. It was the early 1930s. He built the house of steel. It's Streamline Moderne meets Japanese farmhouse. Frank Lloyd Wright and various friends loved this house and often stayed in the smaller front bedroom. Later in his life, among his other cultural contributions, this man introduced Isamu Noguchi to the States and the States to Isamu Noguchi. That was our narrative, and it informed every design decision we made. It trickled down from a small group of people who were in a frenzy to get this house.

The most beautiful family, who happen to be old friends of ours, got the house. The directive was rustic, modern, embrace the Japanese, with a limited palette, and, in particular, with no off-gassing, no indoor air pollution. Small bedrooms and big public spaces was another goal. Promote family activity and limit bedroom time.

Together, we decided we wanted no paint in the house. It was only natural to oil any woods we used and to source responsibly. We quickly limited our palette of materials to hardwoods (to avoid glue and polyurethane and cement) and an experimental clay wall treatment that I had recently read about. Our discussions were centered on a "nonwaste" approach to designing. We were to use what we could that was already on the premises and embrace the spirit of the house. We all wanted the same thing—the seemingly timeless, underdesigned house with roots in a history that was hard to pin to a specific period in time. We call it "no design, design."

The great room has a series of closets under the clerestory windows that houses everything from a deejay setup to a home office, television, and kids' toy closet. The walls are clay. The sliders are wood and the metal window is reclaimed. The floor is a cement tile made to the size and bevel of the original floors. The fireplace is a 1960s classic that we found on one of our "reclaiming" adventures. The rug is Moroccan from Amadi Carpets. The travertine table is by Ten 10 Gallery. The couch and Charlotte Perriand–inspired cabinet are custom-made. The wood side table is by John Williams. The armchair is vintage and was found at Amsterdam Modern.

A large hallway runs the length of the house. To the left is the courtyard and the kitchen, and to the right is the dining room. It's the "spillover" space and very active. Our black porcelain socket was first used there.

There is a wood deck at the back of the house that transitions to the lower garden. Larger dining happens along the built-in benches. The rockers at the outdoor fireplace are by Blackman Cruz.

The essence of this house rests in two places: ground plan and materiality. Ground plan–wise, we consider it Japanese at the core: Most rooms are squares or golden ratios. It's a letter "C" plan that you enter on the long side. To the left of the entry we carved out a master suite and a kids' bedroom. To the right, we had our sacred Frank Lloyd Wright bedroom and a bathroom. In the cavity of the "C" is a pebbled courtyard, our ode to the Noguchi Museum. We made shoji sliders out of American walnut and energy-efficient glass. The kitchen is placed directly opposite the courtyard. It's in the center of the house, open both to the wide hallway and the courtyard beyond and to the dining room and backyard in the other direction. The other end of the "C" holds the great room with windows on all four sides, open to both the courtyard and the backyard. The great room is for everything. Inside those wood closet doors, there is a home office, a television, a deejay setup, and a kids' closet with toys. The kids are not separated—it's all together. This efficient, 1,900-square-foot house has an ideal layout for the modern family. The formal living room is eliminated, the formal dining is outside, passages and gathering spaces are oversize, and all are open to each other. Bedrooms are small. The kitchen is at the heart of the home. Overall, there's a lot of transparency and long views in this now open plan.

< The dining room chairs are vintage Wishbone chairs by Hans Wegner. The table is an early Alma Allen piece that our clients already had. We asked Alma to resize it for this room, and we inlaid brass details. The hanging lantern is by Lawson-Fenning. The patchwork Persian kilim is by Lawrence of La Brea. The bookshelves are oiled walnut.

We opened up the kitchen to the dining room and created a breakfast counter for the kids. The focus was transparency and strong horizontal lines. Notches and simple strips of wood take the place of hardware on the cabinetry. The countertops are a honed slate by Creative Environments, and the cabinetry is all solid walnut. The plates and bowls are a combination of Heath Ceramics and Victoria Morris. The cookie jars are the product of a collaboration we initiated between Alma Allen and Heath.

As far as materiality goes, the concerns about indoor air pollution coupled with the timelessness factor gave us all the answers. We reclaimed old metal windows because you can't tell whether they came with the house or not. They mixed in with existing windows and it was less wasteful. The walls have a thin layer of clay, to avoid painting. The floors are cement tile with a water-based epoxy sealer that prevents off gassing. With the millwork, we carefully planned for expansion, used larger pieces of hardwood, limited hardware, and worked with notches and some joinery to avoid glue. With the exterior of the house, we mixed dirt and stones from the site into the brown coat. It was the most natural and tactile choice, and it tied the structure to the property. With the lighting, we worked with Robert Lewis to design a few custom pieces that were simplified versions of typical lighting. It was also the first time we took a simple workhorse of a light—the porcelain socket—and made it black. It was, again, an underdesigned classic, customized for the house.

The master suite has a simple platform bed and a wall of wood that leads to the closet. The ceiling and walls are again clay. The bed is layered with collected textiles and Matteo sheets. The cabinet is the Lake credenza by BDDW—old and new all mixed up.

The kids' room is one of the most beautiful rooms in the house and is open to the courtyard. It has a custom bunk bed designed by John Williams. The inspiration was a Neutra bunk bed we saw in a nearby house. We needed floor space for playing. The kids have taken over this room and layered it with tons of small collected objects. It's taken on a life of its own.

With the furnishings, we used every bit of what they had: heirlooms, art, small collections of objects, and some key furniture pieces. The rugs throughout are all vintage and wool and have no glue binding them. The couch was born out of a need to seat a lot of people; we wanted a lot of warmth to anchor the room and, of course, we wanted to control the fill and construction methods. It's handmade and filled with wool, wood, metal, and hemp. The kilims gave it instant patina. The side table at the couch was made from leftover wood from the closets. The beloved Alma Allen dining table was resized for its new room. Almost everything else is vintage or handmade in California.

The master bathroom is made out of teak. We used a company in San Francisco to help us source the teak responsibly. The walls are an exterior stucco mix. The tub is custom Corian. The plumbing fixtures are the xo series by Lefroy Brooks. They feel industrial and underdesigned.

We will always be grateful that one of our first experiences doing a house both architecturally and interior design–wise was with such like-minded clients who were willing to take risks and proved time and time again to be the ultimate edit. Whole Foods was still a relatively new phenomenon when we started this project. People were using the word "organic" for everything. "Reclaiming" was unheard of. While the concept honored the history of the house, it is also rooted in our clients' ideals: of consumption, waste, pollution, family life, ways of socializing, and materials that age and patina with life.

The family has grown and in some ways is squeezed into the house. They won't let it go—it's tied to their way of living. For us, that is the most satisfying thing ever. We did our job. It's not about some design aesthetic that is dictated. It's about nurturing and supporting a way of life through design.

One more thing: It turns out there was no Japanese engineer. We've decided that it doesn't matter—the house comes with a new story now.

FARM TO SH

OP TO TABLE

Brentwood photographs by Spencer Lowell   Marin photographs by Mariko Reed   Text by Roman Alonso

Farmshop is the brainchild of chef Jeff Cerciello and his wife, Kira Cunningham, California natives who, after many years of developing projects with chef Thomas Keller, decided to do their own thing. When they approached us in 2009, the local farm-to-table movement was reaching its peak—everyone was doing it—but somehow their ideas stood out to us. In the tradition of iconic restaurants like Chez Panisse, Farmshop serves only locally grown and sourced artisanal product. What sets Farmshop apart is its owners' desire for their environments to look and feel Californian. Jeff and Kira wanted a casual, laid-back atmosphere that exuded a new kind of luxury. They had no interest in referencing French bistros or Italian trattorias. They were looking for interiors all their own and as local, honest, and refined as their food. They didn't know what these interiors should look like, but they had a pretty good idea of what they should feel like. We immediately saw the possibilities. We knew the project presented the opportunity to create a unique aesthetic that combined our love of California-based artisans and craftsmen with Jeff and Kira's commitment to local resources.

Since their first restaurant, located in Brentwood, shares space with a market, creating an elevated and elegant experience was our main challenge. The "luxury" comes from the way things feel rather than the way they look. It's not about decoration; quite the opposite. It's about using the highest quality materials and stripping them down to the most basic elements to create a space that is honest and refined without an ounce of fussiness. All finishes are natural, with no lacquers or sealers. Everything is made to change and acquire a patina with age.

Everything is also made locally. Alma Allen made the tables and bar tops out of silky smooth black walnut and hand-forged metal. Lighting designer Robert Lewis took the macramé lights he created for Ace Palm Springs and turned them into Adolf Loos–inspired chandeliers. Ceramicist Adam Silverman created the hurricane lamps and candle holders. Custom furniture pieces were commissioned from Bolinas-based artisan Trip Carpenter (son of the legend Arthur Espinet Carpenter) and from Michael Boyd in Los Angeles. Heath Ceramics made all the tiles. The uniforms and table linens at the Brentwood location are by Matteo, and the ones at the Marin location come from the San Francisco–based Small Trade Company. A farmer-inspired collage by Los Angeles artist Simon Haas hangs in Brentwood, and a photographic mural by legendary photographer Pirkle Jones, a Mill Valley resident, fills a wall in Marin.

The rooms are elegant but unpretentious, and they feel totally Californian, and in fact they are.

LAMILL COFFEE

coffee	regular or	f	sm	2.²⁵	lg	2.⁷⁵
espresso		sgl	2.⁰⁰	dbl	2.⁵⁰
americano		2.⁷⁵		3.²⁵
cappuccino		3.⁵⁰		4.⁰⁰
macchiato		2.⁵⁰		3.⁰⁰
latte		3.⁵⁰		4.⁰⁰
vanilla or mocha latte		4.⁰⁰		4.⁵⁰
chai latte		3.⁵⁰		3.⁷⁵
hot chocolate		3.²⁵		3.⁷⁵

...OR TEA

h breakfast
rey
jasmine pearl
green moroccan mint
-herbal-   small 3.²⁵
chamomile   large 3.⁷⁵
crimsonberry

inquire about our LAMILL tin program!

The Douglas-fir beams and concrete floor in the Brentwood location were unearthed, exposing the original barnlike structure. All the tables and benches of black walnut and forged steel are by Alma Allen. The chairs are vintage Thonet stripped bare.

The banquettes in Marin are mohair and leather, the sconces are by
Robert Lewis, and the tile—all tile in the place—is by Heath Ceramics.

All casement doors and windows are custom.

The fifty-foot-long walnut bar top and tables are by Alma Allen.
The ceramic candleholders are by Adam Silverman.

In the lounge, the seating is PLANEfurniture by Michael Boyd; the tables are by Trip Carpenter; the stools are by Alma Allen; and the crates are our own. The lamps are Noguchi. The mural is from a photograph by the late photographer and Marin resident, Pirkle Jones.

The pizza oven is unpainted clay.

In the dining room, a rope chandelier by Robert Lewis and a mural from a photograph by Archie Lieberman.

TEXTILES

Our first product under the Commune label was table linens. We took inspiration from the work of Gunta Stölzl and placed metallic stitching on naturally dyed linens made by Matteo right here in Los Angeles. Since we began the line five years ago we've made sleeping bags with Free City, industrial-washed painter's linen throws for Ace, and the softest hemp blankets dyed with leaves, indigo, and flowers with Noon Studio. We are textile obsessed. Our closets are filled with vintage fabrics found on our travels far and wide, and our homes are filled with vintage kilims, as are our clients' homes. There is so much beauty and life and history in these old pieces of rugs. Why not give them another life as a Commune pillow? —Steven Johanknecht

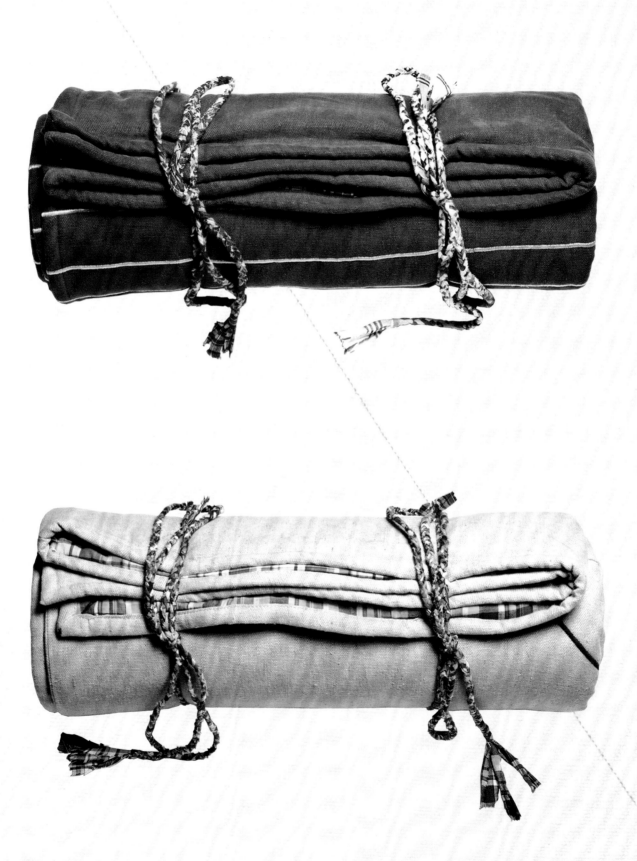

< We worked with Noon Studio on baby-soft hemp blankets dyed with French yellow wildflowers and indigo (top) and with Matteo on plaid linens in Japanese cotton and mattress ticking.

A "nap bag" is a sleeping bag that opens flat to become a bedcover or a picnic blanket; ours were made of naturally dyed linen and Japanese cotton. We made them for Free City in Los Angeles.

Old kilims, rugs, and blankets salvaged and turned into our signature pillows.

A Heath table setting with our linens.

MADE IN CALIFORNIA SINCE 1948

A decade ago, Cathy Bailey and Robin Petravic rescued Heath Ceramics from an uncertain future and became our heroes. By the time our friend, the ceramicist Adam Silverman, suggested we all work together on the first Heath store, they had been at the top of our list of potential collaborators for years. You know the saying, "Never meet your heroes, unless you are ready to be disappointed"? Well, nothing could be further from the truth in this case. Since we started working together in 2007, we have designed and built three stores and worked on a long list of product collaborations that includes dinnerware, clocks, table linens, and the most beautiful canisters made in collaboration with the sculptor Alma Allen. Cathy and Robin are part of our family, and we are always looking for that next opportunity to do something together, so a little chat at their home in Sausalito was a welcome excuse. —*Roman Alonso*

The exterior of the Los Angeles store. We had the paint color custom mixed to match Heath's signature clay.

Roman: How did you end up with Heath?

Cathy: I had driven by the factory before. Back then it looked like a junkyard. I was like, is that Heath? It can't be that mid-century pottery company, it must be something else, 'cause I thought that company didn't exist anymore. You couldn't tell if it was open or not. But we saw someone come out, so we went inside and we couldn't believe it was Heath, the real thing.

Roman: Did you know, the minute you walked in, that it would be yours?

Cathy: Yeah, we knew.

Robin: We sort of looked through the stuff on the tables and the shelves and discovered the quaint price sheet on the wall, which was the only way to figure out how much something cost. We bought a little rim bowl…

Roman: What do you think attracted you about it?

Cathy: I think because we were really dissatisfied with what we were doing at the time, we were ripe for running into something.

Robin: It was like going to a flea market and seeing a piece of furniture and wondering, "Is that a real McCobb?" That's kind of what finding Heath was like as a company; it was unadulterated. You can't pass up something like that; it's so rare.

Roman: Did you immediately have a vision for it or is it something that has evolved?

Cathy: I think we knew the second we walked in the door that the place had good roots and that there was really good design happening there, and most people wouldn't be able to see that.

Robin: We had a vision that's still, I think, pretty intact now. But the business itself has changed a lot over the years. At first we were just going to design things really well and then make them and sell them through distributors. But after a while we couldn't find any great stores. We thought, "This is not gonna work 'cause there's, like, two stores in the whole country."

Cathy: It's true. There was Larry at OK in Los Angeles, and we loved that store, so we thought, we just need to find a Larry in every town.

Roman: Impossible. I mean, it may be easier now.

Robin: We only found a handful.

Cathy: Canoe in Portland, Future Perfect in New York…

Roman: In the end you really needed to create your own culture.

Cathy: In 2003 there were only a few people out there who really understood Heath: Larry; Eric Goode and Sean McPhearson, who had used a lot of the tile at The Maritime; and Roy McMakin… and literally that was it. And nobody was like, "Oh, it's legendary." They knew it was a good thing and that it was still alive, barely, but Heath wasn't a culture. It was a very underground thing.

Robin: And the stores didn't get it at all.

Cathy: They were like, "It's just a little too dated for our customers," like somehow it needed to change.

Robin: They would ask for a special glaze…

Cathy: And they didn't want any brown clay, which is a problem.

Roman: What was the turning point? When did you realize that other people liked it?

Cathy: We showed it to Murray Moss and he loved it and bought a few pieces for his store. He took the classic colors, and of course it didn't look dated at all at Moss; it looked special. So we thought, forget about all these other people, let's make a good line and it'll make its way…

Robin: We didn't do that much; we basically edited some colors out.

Roman: You cleaned up house but continued to work with the same people?

Cathy: All the same people, but there were no designers there; there was nobody to argue with, you know, there was nobody to sell ideas to.

Roman: How was that with you guys coming in?

Cathy: People were relieved and happy because they were worried about their jobs, but then…there were some speed bumps.

Robin: What do you know? Have you ever done pottery? I've been doing pottery for thirty years…that type of thing. We have people that literally have been working in the factory their whole lives, and even Edith Heath's nephew and niece work there.

Roman: But you obviously saw the value in that, as something that kept it really pure.

Cathy: You don't just chop it up. You handle with care. You figure it out…thoughtfully solve the problems.

Roman: In the end that's what we all do, solve problems all day long, every day. That's what design is. People think design is drawing things and handing them off to someone else to make. They don't realize that designing is actually much broader and that it requires you to be quick on your feet and to nurture and mentor people.

Robin: And that's an interesting segue because that's where the whole retail idea came in. It made sense for everything to be connected: the product, the retail, the way we talk about things, the way we treat people who work for us, even the way we wrap product in newspaper at the counter. It's all connected because it's all design. We are designers and we own the company, so who's going to tell us we can't design it all?

Cathy: That leads up to LA. Five years in we were ready to sell stuff that we had designed ourselves the proper way.

Roman: Why LA?

Robin: We always felt the Heath aesthetic had a real affinity with Southern California. So we were drawn to LA.

Cathy: Plus we met Adam [Silverman]. We had been flirting and talking for a while about doing something together. We talked about opening a store, but that wasn't interesting to Adam. We thought maybe he could do a line for Heath, but we didn't have the resources at the time to support that. And then we thought, what about setting up a studio where Adam could do his work and then perhaps some of what he made would find its way into our production, and what if we had a store with the studio to sell his pieces and also Heath. It would be a new model.

Roman: And of course, in a way, that defined your future.

Cathy: And it legitimized what we were doing because it wasn't just about the dishes; it was about the process and it was about the material and then it was about the art of it.

Roman: What made this project so interesting to us was that it was more than just a retail venture. We loved the idea of a pottery studio and gallery and a place to sell this amazing stuff. And especially to visualize it in that location—it wasn't Culver City or Eagle Rock, it was right in the middle of Hollywood. I bet you never expected people would respond the way they did.

Cathy: Did you think it wouldn't work?

Roman: I knew that it would work, but I didn't think that people would be so attracted to it at such an emotional level, that it would become such a culture.

Cathy: We'd hoped it would. What's interesting to me about LA is that the customers feel it is "their" store, that it's somehow independent from Sausalito. I think it's mostly because of the studio and the events held there, but they really connect with the place.

Robin: But this is what we intend with all our stores; we're not trying to create a chain.

Roman: Did you guys have a picture of what the store would look like?

Cathy: No, I was so nervous. When I tried to imagine any designers from San Francisco doing it, I would picture it overdone. I don't know if things are more designed up here or what, but nobody can keep it simple here. So I was scared.

Roman: Simple is hard.

Cathy: And that's what we wanted, and we wanted it to feel real and not fancy. So I knew all those words, but I couldn't design it myself and I didn't know anybody who could.

Roman: What made you think that we could?

Cathy: Adam. He was quite confident. We were worried 'cause we didn't have a lot of money.

Robin: But even if we had eighteen million dollars, we didn't want an eighteen-million-dollar store. It would feel wrong.

Cathy: Adam said he knew who would get it, and he didn't sell it; we were speaking the same language.

The interior of the Los Angeles location. All millwork and fixtures are of knotty pine plywood. We painted the floor a Heath signature blue after it was accidentally ruined while we were trying to seal the original concrete; after five years of wear, it has become one of the most beautiful features of the interior.

< A pine-and-concrete counter houses a refrigerator. The chairs
are powder-coated McMaster-Carr.

A small gallery area leads into the pottery studio in the back.

The interior of the tile factory in San Francisco.

Roman: I think he knew that we'd look out for Heath, that we wouldn't make it about us.

Robin: Do you feel like the stores have the Commune stamp on them?

Roman: Well, what we do for you guys, unlike many of our other clients, definitely resonates with us personally. But our job is really to go into the head of the person we're working with and put together something that perhaps they didn't imagine for themselves but that is really theirs. We're interpreting the information that we gather. With Heath we knew the product and we loved it and we already had it in our homes, all four of us did. In fact we all had been to the factory before we met you, so we immediately knew the concept had to come from there, although it did evolve as we worked together.

Robin: What do you think would be different had you followed your initial instinct?

Roman: I never imagined it being all knotty pine, not in a million years. It would have been redwood. That would have been the obvious. But you know what? That knotty pine is genius, because it's unexpected and the glazes really pop off of it. Plus, it came out of a bunch of concerns, one being that you guys didn't have enough money to use anything else at the time.

Cathy: We had no money at all. And there were those photos you

showed us of the Donald Judd spaces in Marfa.

Roman: Which of course we all love. The whole place is so inspiring. A lot of the detailing on the shelving came from the bookcases in Judd's library.

Cathy: And we had just been to Marfa, so we thought, OK, we can totally trust this one.

Roman: I remember there were very few references in your presentation because we had to do it so quickly, but it just flowed.

Cathy: I don't think we had any choices, did we? It was kind of like, this is what we think.

Roman: I remember we came up to the factory, and we looked at it very carefully. We photographed everything you loved and hated about it. We really made a study and got a good sense of what the experience of shopping Heath should feel like, and that, actually, is the best way for us to work, when the client lets us figure out how it should feel rather than how it should look. You were able to go with a feeling rather than visuals, and that doesn't happen all the time.

Robin: We work very differently from other designers; we're both more like managers—our first instinct is not to sit down with a pencil. When we work with a designer, we let them do their work and then ask the right questions.

Roman: And you have to trust that the designer is going to take it beyond where you left off and that they're gonna come back to you. And that the design is going to be what you thought it could be, or they're going to surprise you in a really delightful way.

Cathy: Can you believe it's been five years since it opened this December?

Roman: How do you feel about it now?

Cathy: It's broken in now, and everything's super warm, and it's so good. It feels like it's been there forever.

Roman: It feels like it's had a nice, little life. It's aged exactly how we hoped it would. It's just so honest; it is what it is. And that's really hard because we used very inexpensive materials, which you have to finish and detail a certain way so they evolve nicely.

Cathy: Like the floors?

Roman: The floor is amazing. It was such a disaster with the floors at first but even that, in the end, turned into a blessing in disguise.

Cathy: It's beautiful, that blue. It's starting to wear through to the red that's underneath.

Robin: How do you feel about how the space is being used now?

Roman: I love that the courtyard became part of the studio and that it's more useful, that it's not just a pretty space. I feel that using every inch of it is where it's at. It's not precious, but it's visual.

Robin: It's a little bit more like the design of our building in San Francisco.

Roman: It became a full reality in San Francisco: the idea of manufacturing, showing, and selling, all in the same environment. LA was a little prototype for that.

Robin: Have you ever read *How Buildings Learn*, by Stewart Brand? He did the *Whole Earth Catalog*. It's about how buildings start out as one thing, but if you allow for life to take place there, they become something else. That freedom is so important. So the way that Adam just one day opened that door we had sealed and there it was, an outdoor studio…

Roman: We couldn't have planned that. In the beginning it was about having event space, but that really wasn't the best use of the space. I guess that's how we all learn best, right? On the job.

Robin: It's become our signature…learning as we go. We try to figure everything out far in advance, but if a better idea pops up along the way we just go for it.

Roman: And yet somehow you have a 60,000-square-foot factory in the middle of San Francisco. In the case of that space, did you immediately have a vision for it?

Robin: We couldn't wrap our heads around it at first.

Cathy: It was such a mess; the floor was terrible and there were all these elevation issues, a total nightmare, but somehow we knew that with all that amazing light it would all be OK.

Roman: Do you think you'll open another place?

Cathy: Well, people keep asking for one on the East Coast. About 25 percent of our business is there. If we had a really good store, it'd probably be a good business, but then again, what's wrong with being just in California?

Roman: Nothing. Some things don't travel.

Cathy: And we'd have to work there all the time. We like New York, but not all the time. A New York apartment? We don't need that.

Roman: People always say to us [Commune], "You should open an office in New York. You would have so much business there." And it's like, well, we already have business in New York without being there—how much more do we need?

Robin: It's like saying you should clone yourself because then you could do twice as much stuff as you do now.

Roman: I can barely deal with one of me; I can't imagine dealing with two. But there's comfort in knowing that you could. That's part of growing up: You never say never.

Cathy: Don't slam the door…

Robin: Always leave the door open.

The exterior of the factory/store/studio/gallery in San Francisco.

The demonstration kitchen leads to a gallery area with retail and factory beyond.

< The demonstration kitchen has copper countertops.

The interior of the tile showroom in San Francisco.

The entrance to the factory and retail area in San Francisco.

LIVING SMALL

Steven Johanknecht and I have been friends and colleagues for twenty-five years. As long as we've known each other, we've lived in small spaces in both New York City and Los Angeles, and yet we love objects and art and books and furniture and textiles. The sizes of our homes have never limited the size of our collections. There is an art to living small. For the first time in all the years we've known each other, we sat down in his Silver Lake cottage to talk about it. —*Roman Alonso*

Roman: Do you think that we like living in these little places because of our time living in New York or is it just that we don't want to have room for anyone else but ourselves?

Steven: Maybe a little bit of both. (Laughs)

R: You had a tiny place in New York.

S: My condo was close to 700 square feet. They called it a junior one-bedroom. What attracted me to it was the layout. It was super efficient.

R: What was it that attracted you to your cottage here in LA? What was the first thing?

S: Well, it was so cute. But I think the flow, the layout. It just seemed like the perfect fit.

R: Do you think when living in a small place it helps if you have a lot of different little rooms? My apartment is 800 square feet, but it has, like, seven rooms. I think it would feel a lot smaller if it were one 800-square-foot room.

S: Yeah, I think that's true. Here I have a very dark, little cozy den that opens to a tiny courtyard and then into a small painting studio. I get to have all of these different experiences, but I get to enjoy them all because this place is so small.

R: Exactly. That's what's really great, that there's no waste. I don't understand when two people live in a 10,000-square-foot house. I'm, like, scared of it. Why would I maintain 10,000 square feet when I don't need them? Nobody needs 10,000 square feet; they might want them, but they don't need them.

S: Well, the other thing is, in a small space you're closer to the things you love and collect. If you have empty rooms that you don't go into, they become just storage or a museum.

R: Well, even if you have lots of big rooms that are full of stuff, they're still like a museum. You can live in only so much space before the rest becomes just extra.

S: Quentin Crisp lived in a studio apartment until the day he died. And he said, "You can only be in one room at a time."

R: How true is that?

S: After I moved to California, it felt like such a luxury to have a couple of extra rooms. But I don't feel the need for more. I think there is a luxury to a smaller space.

R: It's definitely a luxury. My biggest luxury today is the luxury of time, right? So a small house affords you the luxury of time. It's just logical that it would be a more luxurious experience because it's not sucking the life out of you. And in the end it's how you fill it, what it feels like, what it smells like. That's what creates luxury. It's not the amount of space, per se. I think there are plenty of big houses that are supposed to be luxurious, but they aren't. They are fancy. They are over-the-top but not necessarily luxurious.

S: I'm amazed at how a small space can sort of eat up things and how you can layer on a life. You're engaged on a very close level with everything you have. So your collections are made up of only what you love.

R: You brought a lot of stuff from New York, didn't you?

S: Everything.

R: I didn't. I brought only three pieces of furniture. I still have that Danish table I bought on Bond Street.

S: Your Bertoia chair.

R: Yeah, and the Paul McCobb cabinet, and I brought the Kem Weber chair. Those are the only things I brought. But I sure accumulated shit fast when I got here! It's like the land of accumulation in LA—such great stuff to have...everywhere.

S: I think that because I lived in a modernist high-rise in New York, everything felt different when I got here. I was able to appreciate the pieces in a different way, seeing them in a place that was a completely different style.

R: Well, you always had really good stuff, so why would you get rid of it just because you were leaving New York?

(*continued on page 139*)

Roman in the coat closet he converted into a library. The chair is a vintage Hans Wegner. The stool is a cut-to-fit wood block inside a Free City decorated gift box.

< The living room rugs are from India, early twentieth century, and came from the estate of Tony Duquette. On them sit a vintage 1920s Kem Weber chair, a walnut Alma Allen stool with two of his bronze sculptures, a Douglas-fir prototype for Commune crates, and Commune vintage kilim floor pillows.

The built-in redwood buffet and paneling are original to the house. A vintage dining table and chairs and a Noguchi lamp sit on the Egyptian rug. The prints are part of Roman's Cuban art collection.

<< The sofa is an early prototype from the Commune for Environment line; it's a simple mattress and box spring upholstered in painter's linen. The photography is by Dennis Hopper, Lisa Eisner, Wallace Berman, Eikoh Hosoe, and Pirkle Jones, among others. The reading light is a prototype by Robert Lewis for the "Love" lights created for the Ace Hotel in Palm Springs.

In the sleeping porch there is another upholstered daybed, this one covered in sheep skin. The Bertoia Diamond chair has its original upholstery. Artwork and photographs are by Konstantin Kakanias, Ron Galella, Mike Brodie, Vaginal Davis, and Alexander Girard.

Original Cuban film posters from the 1960s and 1970s and Fillmore
posters hang in the kitchen, along with a cowboy print by Lisa Eisner.

The bed is covered with a Commune/Free City nap bag and vintage Japanese fabrics. The pillows are Commune vintage kilim pillows. The photograph is by Jeff Burton.

PHOTOGRAPHS BY WILLIAM ABRANOWICZ

(*continued from page 127*)

S: When you move you end up keeping only the things you love, and then maybe it goes through an awkward stage because it's in a different place, but if you love it, you keep it and add things that work with it and evolve perhaps in a different direction. But you also appreciate your past. You're not just tossing everything out.

R: Well, you have to be really careful, and you have to edit. You have to think about it when you're about to buy something. The only things I don't think about at all, that I just buy, are books. I don't care how many books I have. They can go anywhere. And for years they were all over the house. That closet-turned-library was a life changer. I don't want to have storage spaces. As it is, I have shit everywhere. I have shit in your house. I have shit at the office. If I acquired more stuff, I'd have to get another house. At one point, we shared a two-bedroom house in LA that wasn't that big, and all our stuff was in there together and it looked great.

S: I think our stuff mixed well together. It taught us that if what you collect is truly of a personal nature it will always mix well with another person's collection, and that's important to know if you have to share a small space with someone.

R: Now, tell me about this house. What is it?

S: It's part of a cluster of little writers cottages built by Disney Studios in 1928 in the style of Snow White and the Seven Dwarfs.

R: Which, of course, is so perfect for LA.

S: They were planned really well; living room, dining, and kitchen are one area, there's a den and a small laundry room, and two small courtyards. The bedroom was added later in the attic. I knew the minute I saw it. It felt right.

R: That's pretty old for LA. Mine's from 1908, so it's more than one hundred years old, which in LA is, like, ancient. It's like living in the Coliseum or something.

S: But the plan is so great because you have that rhythm of rooms from a reading porch all the way through to the bedroom.

R: At 800 square feet, I have a laundry room. Can you imagine in New York having your own laundry room?

S: No.

R: And here you've got also the outdoors, which of course helps. It's a little space, but you've got a lot of light, which in New York you don't necessarily have.

S: I think with a smaller space it's also about not being afraid of layering. You start with a good couch, a good table, and chairs—things that are large that you love and that mean something to you. And the items that surround it are what you layer on. Hang art on your walls gallery style...

R: Or stack everything on the floor three or four deep like I do.

S: Setting up a small space to work well is really pleasurable.

R: You're actually creating a life. It's not that different from what we help our clients do—helping them create the physical representation of their lives.

S: I think sometimes it's rough for clients if their house is too big. They're trying to get a sense of home and comfort in their environment, and it's hard to do if you're approaching a massive property all at once.

R: Comfort is a really good word. Everybody wants comfort, and yet large spaces can be really uncomfortable in many different ways. It can be physically uncomfortable. It can be emotionally uncomfortable. It can even be mentally uncomfortable. So comfort doesn't necessarily come with the big size.

S: I think sometimes people think only about real estate. They don't think about how important it is for their environment to enhance their lives. A home should be nurturing, no matter what size it is. But people, particularly in this town, tend to lose sight of that.

R: Well, I guess to some people size is a symbol of success. It can be cultural.

S: People can be afraid of small spaces if they don't know what to do with them. You tell people, "Don't be afraid of large furniture in a small space." I mean, I have a nine-foot credenza in my attic bedroom. It was a bitch to get up there, but it makes the room feel great to have that massive piece of furniture in there.

R: Another one is dark color. It's funny how people are so afraid of dark colors in a small space, but sometimes it actually makes the space look bigger because you can push it far enough that it comes back in the other direction. I say never be afraid of small. It's all about adjustment.

S: A good home is like a good suit—it's always about the fit. Sometimes a small space is the perfect size, and the pleasure of a home where you use and enjoy every room is a way of living a luxurious life surrounded by what you love and the life you have collected.

Steven Johanknecht in the courtyard of his 1928 Tudor-style cottage.

‹ An Alma Allen metal-and-walnut coffee table flanked by vintage metal chairs. The hanging bronze bells are by Paolo Soleri and the multifaced ceramic sculpture is by Howard Whalen.

In the living room, a stainless steel and white leather Mies van de Rohe chair and a prototype Commune for Environment coffee table. The fireplace screen is a Commune design and the wall sconce is by Arne Jacobsen.

A vintage Danish ladderback chair sits next to a rosewood chest by George Tanier. The painting is Italian from the 1950s. The walnut stool is by Alma Allen.

> In the dining room a Gaetano Sciolari chandelier hangs above a solid walnut table designed by Steven, surrounded by dining chairs by Peter Hvidt. The lithographs are by David Storey. The pine-log side chair is by Sabena.

In the kitchen, the chandelier is vintage French cast iron; on the open shelves sit Heath Ceramic dinnerware, and the plate on the wall is Fornasetti.

> The deep green of the den is a custom color mixing Chrome Green and Pacific Teal by Benjamin Moore. The upholstered daybed is covered in Belgian linen and has a corduroy bolster, and the vintage kilim pillows are by Commune. The brass-top table is an original prototype for Commune crates in Douglas fir. On the wall are prints by Richard Prince, Peter Max, and Cindy Sherman.

< In the attic bedroom, the bed is vintage George Nelson, the chair is by Verner Panton, and the stool is by Alma Allen. On the zebrawood credenza sits a Memphis "Super" lamp by Martine Bedin.

The garage was converted into a painting studio that opens to a small walled garden.

Richard Burton

Sang Here.

Photographs by Richard Powers · Text by Mayer Rus

First appeared in *Architectural Digest*, January 2013. Rus / *Architectural Digest* © Condé Nast.

Richard Burton and Judy Garland belt it out in the anteroom, as captured by Jean Howard, 1953. The entry foyer had lost some of its Spanish Colonial roots, so we installed a wood ceiling and stenciled around the light canopy. The bench is Mexican Colonial from the Yucatán. The console table is cast bronze by Blackman Cruz. The front door is all Billy Haines.

When Dinah and Bill Ruch purchased their residence in Los Angeles' Coldwater Canyon two years ago, they had no idea that a rich tapestry of Hollywood history had unfolded there. "We saw pictures of the house, and I said, 'Let's get in the car and buy it,'" recalls Bill, a retired entrepreneur. "We loved the indoor-outdoor feeling and Spanish Colonial details like the terra-cotta roof." His wife, who serves as board president for LA's Levitt Quinn Family Law Center, adds, "We honestly didn't know anything about the previous owners. It was the lush landscape and the courtyard fountain that sealed the deal."

Hollywood may be littered with pedigreed properties, but few are as steeped in delicious Tinseltown lore as this home (previously featured in the June 1978 issue of *Architectural Digest*). Built in 1935, it later belonged to Charles K. Feldman and Jean Howard. Feldman, a powerful talent agent, managed the careers of Lauren Bacall, Howard Hawks, John Wayne, and other industry titans while also producing such noteworthy movies as *A Streetcar Named Desire* and *The Seven Year Itch*. Howard, a famous beauty and former Ziegfeld girl, came to LA as an aspiring actress and rose to prominence as a legendary hostess and a photographer of the entertainment world.

Feldman and Howard bought the house in 1942, and following a renovation by silent-film star turned decorator William Haines, a pioneer of Hollywood Regency style, it became the backdrop for fabled parties, assignations, and assorted debaucheries. Humphrey Bogart, Marlene Dietrich, and Greta Garbo were among the pair's frequent guests. Elia Kazan and Marilyn Monroe carried on an affair in one of the bedrooms while Arthur Miller typed away by the pool, plotting his own seduction of the screen siren. In 1960, when John F. Kennedy arrived for the Democratic National Convention, Feldman and Howard hosted a soiree to introduce the future president to the cream of the movie business. Details of that evening are sketchy, but by most accounts a good time was had by all.

After the Ruchs acquired the home, they called on a longtime family friend, Pamela Shamshiri of the LA interior design firm Commune, to revive the place. It was Shamshiri who unearthed the property's storied past, which the couple eagerly embraced. "Bill and Dinah really wanted to bring the house back to its roots," she explains. "I had to figure out how to do something that was fundamentally Spanish Colonial in style but still acknowledged the Billy Haines interiors, which included incredible custom pieces by Tony Duquette."

The 5,000-square-foot, four-bedroom structure had retained only vestigial traces of its Spanish Colonial and Hollywood Regency heritage. "It was a mishmash," Shamshiri says. "All the walls were painted white, every room had a different floor, and there was a strange French-style kitchen." Fulfilling an important client directive, she combined three poky cooking and pantry areas into a single expansive kitchen. It now features two islands, green-painted cabinets (some with copper-mesh fronts), and a fluted hood. To accentuate the Spanish character, she incorporated dark-stained Douglas-fir ceiling beams, a strategy also employed in the main hallway.

The fireplace wall of the living room is covered in antique mirror as it was in the Billy Haines era. The fireplace and crown molding were restored. The chairs belonged to our clients. The painting on the mantle is by filmmaker Jean Negulesco; it's a nod to the Modigliani that used to hang in this legendary party room.

> The plan in the living room is directly from the Billy Haines design. As the doors open, the chandelier turns on automatically and two L-shaped sofas with bookcases above unfold on each side. The room was originally a deep green. The rug is a Commune hex rug in hemp and silk. The lamps are original Billy Haines.

References to the historic Haines scheme become more overt in the living and dining areas, where Shamshiri relied on archival photographs and commissioned on-site excavations to determine the original wall colors. In the living room, restored to a deep sage-green, she kept Haines's expanse of antiqued-mirror panels around the fireplace, as well as his banquette-seating configuration and built-in bookshelves—though she added a discreet television enclosure. A portrait by the filmmaker Jean Negulesco is displayed prominently above the carved mantel, while vintage Duquette table lamps in the shape of Buddha heads now flank the room's double doors, setting the tone for the glamorous yet inviting space.

Shamshiri created a curving copper-top bar for the compact sitting room, where sparkling conversation still flows as freely as the cocktails and cigarettes once did. She even installed a piano in the same spot where Judy Garland serenaded Richard Burton—a moment captured in a Howard photograph that hangs nearby on a plaster wall stenciled by decorative artist Nic Valle in a pattern of faded black florets. "The Ruchs entertain all the time, so it made sense to keep that bubbly spirit alive," Shamshiri says.

Working within the existing footprint, the designer reconfigured the master suite to provide separate his-and-her studies—the latter embellished with a trellis mural by Valle. Shamshiri also gave the couple a luxurious new master bath, outfitted with Moroccan tiles by Ann Sacks, a freestanding tub, and Italian reverse-painted glass sconces that once graced the tearoom at London's Fortnum & Mason department store.

Outdoors, Shamshiri and her clients agreed to do only cosmetic upgrades, leaving the pool and courtyard intact to preserve their palpable sense of Hollywood history. They also left two guest rooms off the kitchen—one of which may or may not have been the site of a presidential tryst—largely as they found them. "Pam really taught us to appreciate everything that had gone on in this house," Bill says. "Frankly, I love the idea that my den was the original den of iniquity."

"I had to figure out how to do something that was fundamentally Spanish Colonial in style but still acknowledged the Billy Haines interiors," Shamshiri says.

We call this the anteroom because it's where you can play and listen to the piano and have a drink at the bar before the doors to the living room are opened. We stenciled the walls in black and white to support the transition into both the green living room and the red dining room. The furnishings are all vintage.

< The kitchen was originally four rooms that we combined into one grand space. We also opened up the archway to the greenhouse breakfast room. The tiles throughout are custom, and the countertops are oiled walnut.. All the lighting is by Paul Ferrante.

In the spirit of old Hollywood 1930s glamour, the study is "trellised" and has painted vines growing through it. There is a mural of Mount Tamalpais to one side. All the decorative painting throughout the house was done by Nic Valle, who is a Hollywood legend himself.

The master bathroom was originally two bathrooms that were combined into one. The pedestal sinks and plumbing fixtures are by Lefroy Brooks. The bathtub is by Waterworks. The wainscot tile is a Moroccan mosaic. The trim throughout is marble and all the walls have antique mirrors.

The four-poster bed in the master bedroom is a family heirloom. The bench at the foot of the bed is by George Smith. The rug is by The Rug Company. All the bedding is by Matteo.

FURNITURE

About seven years ago, in our old studio at 666 Robertson, we were lucky enough to have our own workshop run by a very talented artist, John Williams. In that workshop we began the process of creating the language of what would become Commune's first furniture collection handmade in the United States by Environment. Unlike the interiors we do for our clients, this process was not about them. It was about us and the furniture we want for ourselves and in all of our projects. With a nod to heroes like Donald Judd and Wendell Castle, Commune furniture—simple, honest, and built to last from naturally finished materials—is meant to age and be loved for a long, long time...and to move with you as your environments, experiences, and life change. — Steven Johanknecht

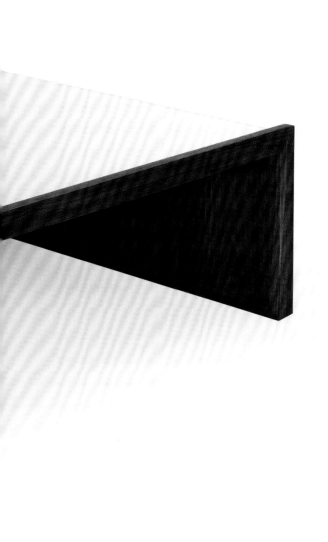

Coffee table of solid black walnut with copper band, brass flat-head screw detail, and bronze mirror.

Cleat sofa of solid black walnut and painters' linen upholstery.

Cleat dining chairs in solid walnut, with a painters' linen seat and
a shearling cover (opposite) that comes off in the summer.

Our daybed. We wanted to create something sexy and simple;
it rests directly on the floor with an attitude of dorm room meets
Paris nightclub. In shearling and painters' linen.

It started with a box: simple boxes with a brass cleat to lock them together into multiple configurations. We started with a brass or solid-wood top and later evolved the design language to include storage. We went vertical, we added brass cubes...the collection continues to grow and we love it mixed up.

The dining table has a "split" base lined in copper and a brass foot.

We simplified the living room fireplace down to plaster and tile. The tile is original to the house. The "lipstick" andirons are vintage from the 1960s. The sconces are French from the 1940s and the Sunburst mirror is a new piece by Blackman Cruz. We even made stationery for this house based on the tile pattern from the kitchen.

Spanish Modern

Photographs by Corey Walter & Lisa Romerein
Text by Ramin Shamshiri

When we first saw the house in the Los Feliz area of Los Angeles, we were taken by the homes in the neighborhood and its picturesque hillside landscape. It offered an escape, just minutes from a bustling metropolis. The home's layout was clean and simple and had an abundance of balconies and terraces that opened onto a beautiful garden, as well as onto views of the city, canyon, and ocean. It did not have an authentic aura about it, but it still felt like a quintessential Los Angeles house, albeit one buried behind decades of remodeling. The house was built in 1926 with Moorish undertones but felt Spanish in its intention.

The house had its issues. The floor plan would have flowed nicely if not for the misalignment of doors and archways. There was an excessive amount of artificial stone in the entry and stairway, track and recessed lighting throughout, glossy textured-stucco walls, balconies covered with either modern tiles or roofing materials, and a kitchen from the eighties that had great light but little else to recommend it. All of these elements detracted from the home's historical feel, or even that it was built eighty-seven years ago. We wanted to create a better flow, while accentuating the home's Moorish tones, and introduce elements that inspired us on recent trips to Argentina and that recalled the haciendas of Mérida, Mexico.

In many ways, we did little more than bring the house back to its roots, where it belonged. While this required addressing all elements of the house, the process came so naturally that it often seemed like we did nothing; guests often remark on the fact. It's arguably the most flattering compliment we've received. We replaced the artificial stone floors with wood, widened and lined up the archways, smoothed out the textured walls with a skim coat of plaster, coved ceilings in the dining room and bedrooms, removed all recessed and track lighting, stripped and stained all doors and windows with a dark walnut finish, replaced any casement windows with traditional wood-framed, mullioned windows, re-covered the balconies with period tiles, and gave the house a paint job appropriate to the era. All of this created what felt like a home built in 1926, and allowed us the liberty to have fun with the furnishings.

In our residential projects, we want everything that is part of the architecture or attached to the building, excluding lights, to feel authentic and appropriate to the style and era in which the house was built. We express the character and personalities of our clients through the furnishings. This approach is respectful of the architecture while allowing the owners to change elements over time as their tastes and personalities inevitably evolve.

As you enter the house through the glass and iron front door, you encounter a large petrified wooden stump that dominates the foyer. To the left is a George Smith sofa and above that a wood ceiling restored to a dark walnut stain and anchored by a 1960s glass light fixture. We revamped the stairwell to include new ironwork and handrails inspired by a Yucatanian design. We aligned the archways on either side of the foyer and made them wider and circular to recall the romance of the era.

The living room floor is covered with a large hide rug from Grand Splendid. The coffee table by Commune is centered in the room, surrounded by a red custom sofa from Dana John, a pair of vintage Sergio Rodrigues arm chairs found at Brenda Antin, and a large bench by Arthur Casas. On the wall is a large Massimo Vitali photograph that feels more like a window onto the Mediterranean. We rounded and widened another large archway, off the living room, that invites you into the family room, which features a ten-foot sofa by Monteverdi-Young covered in bright yellow fabric. This sofa, combined with a George Smith ottoman and the classic Eames lounge chair covered in an ikat fabric, makes the family room a great place to relax and watch movies.

The dining room has a patchwork hide rug under a large custom marble dining table. A great super-realist, almost pop art, still-life painting by Douglas Bond radiates various hues of orange into the room. This room catches beautiful sunrises to the east behind downtown Los Angeles through sheer curtains made from a Missoni fabric. A large vintage door salvaged from an old church slides across, closing off the kitchen from the dining room when necessary.

The old church door that separates the kitchen from the dining room is rarely closed because the view through to the kitchen captures the style and tone of the house. In the kitchen, we gutted everything and removed the former butler's pantry to create one open space. We painted the cabinets the same dark green that we saw on all exterior doors in a village in Argentina. We widened the opening to the courtyard between the family room and the kitchen and carried the custom cement tile from the kitchen out to the courtyard to make the spaces feel connected. We increased the height of the walls in the courtyard and added planters at the top to create the feeling of a Moorish sunken garden. We also added the fireplace, by Stan Bitters, and a fountain. The table in the courtyard is from Ten 10 and the chairs are from Brown Jordan. In the end, these two areas tied the house together and are the common gathering points for every meal from casual breakfasts to formal thirty-person dinners.

Finally, one of our favorite rooms is the small office upstairs, which is dominated by a large red Donald Judd partners desk flanked by brown-leather aluminum-group Eames chairs. There is a patchwork rug and some simple shelving and drapery. The room sits on the southeast corner of the house, which has a wraparound balcony with a hammock and some lounging chairs. While the house was under construction, we would often do site visits after-hours and surprise the crew and their significant others taking in the spectacular view with a bottle of wine. To the southwest, Hollywood turns into West Los Angeles, which eventually rolls into the beautiful blues of the Pacific Ocean. To the southeast is the skyline of downtown Los Angeles, with the beautiful City Hall overshadowed by the towering skyscrapers of Bunker Hill. To the east the rolling landscape of the Santa Monica Mountains lies in the foreground, with the San Gabriel Mountains hovering behind. Sitting out there, you realize this is why you live in Los Angeles—for that array of inspiration that comes from the juxtaposition of a variety of natural and human-made landscapes. All of it basks in an abundance of sunshine or glimmering city lights; there is so much to take in, the only hard part is deciding which scene to enjoy.

The pointed windows of the living room were one of the few "Spanish" elements left in the house after a 1980s renovation. These windows are the inspiration for all the Moorish details in the house, including the coves we added to help with the low ceilings. The furniture is an eclectic mix of South American modern (the Sergio Rodrigues armchairs), Hollywood glamour (custom tufted sofa), Persian and Turkish textiles, and new (bench by Arthur Casas).

< The den is an arched alcove off the living room where we tucked in a very long Monteverdi-Young sofa upholstered in bright yellow linen on one side and a television on the other. The ceiling of this room is wallpapered in rattan. The ottoman is a classic George Smith blanket box. The rug is from the Atlas Mountain region in Morocco.

The Eames chair is covered in an ikat fabric. The abstract painting is by Steven Johanknecht, and was a housewarming gift.

< The Donald Judd desk anchors the home office. The desk chairs are vintage Eames Aluminum Group chairs in leather. The curtains are a simple burlap with traditional details. The rug is a patchwork of Persian kilims.

The marble dining room table was custom-made and craned into the room. The leather dining room chairs are nineteenth-century Spanish. The chandelier is by Paul Ferrante.. The curtains are Missoni and the custom valances were made to not only add more "Spanish" to the room but also to help with the ceiling and window heights. The wood door is a fourteenth-century Argentinean church door.

For the kitchen we combined three rooms, and we widened the opening to the courtyard and added a bifold door between the rooms. The courtyard was raised to the level of the kitchen, and we made a custom cement tile for both spaces to tie the two together. The full-height, smaller subway tiles help modernize the space. The cabinets are all inset in the "pre-war" style. We added an arch to the doors, used a classic Spanish green, and installed walnut countertops.

> We achieved a sunken-courtyard feeling by raising the perimeter walls by seven feet and adding planters at the top of the walls so that the vines would grow downward to form a screen blocking the neighbors from view. The outdoor fireplace anchors the space and has a Stan Bitters ceramic wall mural. The outdoor dining room table is travertine, and the chairs are vintage Dan Johnson.

The courtyard has a fountain made of hand-cut Moroccan tile and cast cement pieces. The spout is reclaimed from a mosque. The alligator is vintage, and the black lantern is Oaxacan.

> We deliberately made the fireplace slightly shallow so that black soot from the smoke would coat and accentuate the ceramic tiles, much like in old adobes. The Stan Bitters fireplace is surrounded by French 1950s garden furniture. The travertine table is a new piece by Ten 10 Gallery.

COME IN, WE'RE OPEN. adventures in retail design

We approach the design of a retail space in much the same personalized way as we do the design of someone's house: It is a home for a collection. A store or showroom needs to reflect the client and live on beyond a particular product season or trend; it is a significant aspect of defining who they are. We try to establish timeless designs, consider existing architecture, and create an environment that evolves with the client. — *Steven Johanknecht*

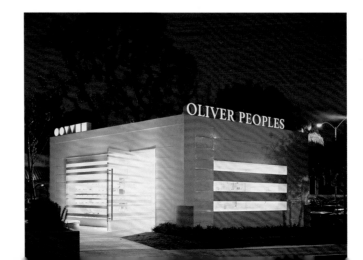

OLIVER PEOPLES

Our first store for Oliver Peoples (OP) was a freestanding flagship located in the Malibu country mart. The goal was to create a new environment for the brand that could be a template for all future stores. We started looking at the simplicity of the OP logo and the strong graphic shapes. We established a palette of signature materials: white powder-coated metal, unfinished ash, clear mirror, and simple concrete floors. There is a strong relationship between the exterior and interior of the store with simple, strong horizontal bands running throughout. Eyeglasses are presented on inset shelves with pause points along the wall of blocks of mirror. The store has a quality of lightness and simplicity and is a great backdrop for trying on new frames without visual distraction. Natural light floods the space. A large, wide, low counter serves as the cash wrap and features a variety of stools by the artist Alma Allen, which add a sculptural element. There is also a small desk with Eames chairs for personal fitting and adjustments. Magazines, books, music selections, and iPod stations are integrated. We've designed three stores for Oliver Peoples, including a mall location and a Madison Avenue flagship. They now use our design as a template for their own.

Photographs by Corey Walter

HOLLYWOOD
TRADING
COMPANY

Hollywood Trading Company specializes in denim, small collections, and a huge selection of belts. They have vintage and new collections, and we created a design about contrast. In a narrow space, a ceiling and sidewall made entirely of reclaimed wood interface with a smooth white wall and a high-gloss, painted white floor. We designed polished-chrome linear light fixtures that hang down, shining up on the wood ceiling. One long light cove illuminates the junction of the two contrasting material worlds. One long fixture inspired by an Eames cabinet sits on legs along the white wall, while the reclaimed wood wall has adjustable hardware integrated within the wood panels. Found rugs and flea market finds are sprinkled around. The cash counter is a simple, yellow powder-coated metal box that juts out into the space from the back, creating the only blast of color other than the merchandise and displays. The façade is all glass with a large, wood door handle carved by the artist Alma Allen.

Photographs by Corey Walter

Our first store for Undefeated, a hip store for well-edited footwear and clothing, is located in Silverlake. Our first move was to paint the exterior of the entire strip mall black. Some tenants weren't happy at first. But now everyone loves it. We exposed the wood ceiling and suspended linear fluorescent lights. Lights continue out to the exterior. We wanted the entire space to be bright at all times. We designed one long line of simple shelving leaning against the wall and featuring running shoes. The effect recalls bleacher seating. One large ottoman is covered in basketball leather and rests on deep-blue, wall-to-wall carpet that runs throughout the space. The large cash wrap counter is painted in automotive paint and features the store's own super graphic as a backdrop.

Photographs by Corey Walter

UNDEFEATED

As if Dior had been born in California! We created a small boutique for a special tailored men's clothing label based in Los Angeles. The walls of the narrow space are clad in brass that is sealed in a subdued finish somewhere between polished and antiqued. The panels reflect the clothes and provide the room with depth. Simple hang bars present the clothing in museum-like simplicity, and shelves of Claro walnut display folded clothes. Strong linear lighting runs front to back, and plants in geometric metal planters hang below skylights in the center of the store. There is a carved wood table and stools by Alma Allen. The main dressing area is a cozy room with full-height velvet drapes, a fireplace, and upholstered seating.

Photographs by Spencer Lowell

MATTISON

THE STANDARD

The store at the Standard Hotel in New York City feels like a perfect little international magazine and sundry shop. It's almost hard to tell whether the shop was always there and the hotel was built up around it or the other way around—it's tucked away behind the lobby, with a side entrance. A wall has display niches of various sizes painted a deep red and features brass vitrines and card-catalog drawers for gum, candy, condoms, toothpaste, and so on. A graphic, cement tile floor runs throughout with tambour wood walls and a copper-wrapped column, there is built-in seating along the windows, and a ceiling is dropped in the center and features in high-gloss paint a large geometric graphic inspired by Gio Ponti.

Photographs by Spencer Lowell

KIKI
DE
MONTPARNASSE

Kiki is a store for luxury lingerie, erotic gifts and toys, art, and books. The right store design was essential. It was important to make the spaces in New York and LA elegant and comfortable for both men and women shoppers. It had to set just the right tone to avoid being crass or sleazy. The stores were designed as a sequence of rooms painted in three shades of mauve, from lightest to darkest, and the last room has plush wall-to-wall carpet. Ring chandeliers define the rooms and simultaneously evoke both a palace and a circus. Fitting rooms behind heavy curtains are generous and accommodate a guest (or two or three). The lighting can be controlled to affect "before and after." Natural burlap curtains can be used to conceal the display window from the street; the rough texture is in sharp contrast to the silk and feathers on the custom-colored mannequins.

Photographs by Lisa Eisner

FLOORED

Our Signet Collection of flooring is a collaboration with Exquisite Surfaces. Reclaimed French oak floors are custom dyed in three signature colors; Indigo, Sand, and Army. The finishing touch is a trademark brass signet created for us by E. R. Butler & Co. Our graphic Bauhaus parquet floors are fully modular and are inspired by geometric designs from Latvian textiles. You can imagine them in a huge eighteenth-century building in Copenhagen or in a Manhattan loft. — *Steven Johanknecht*

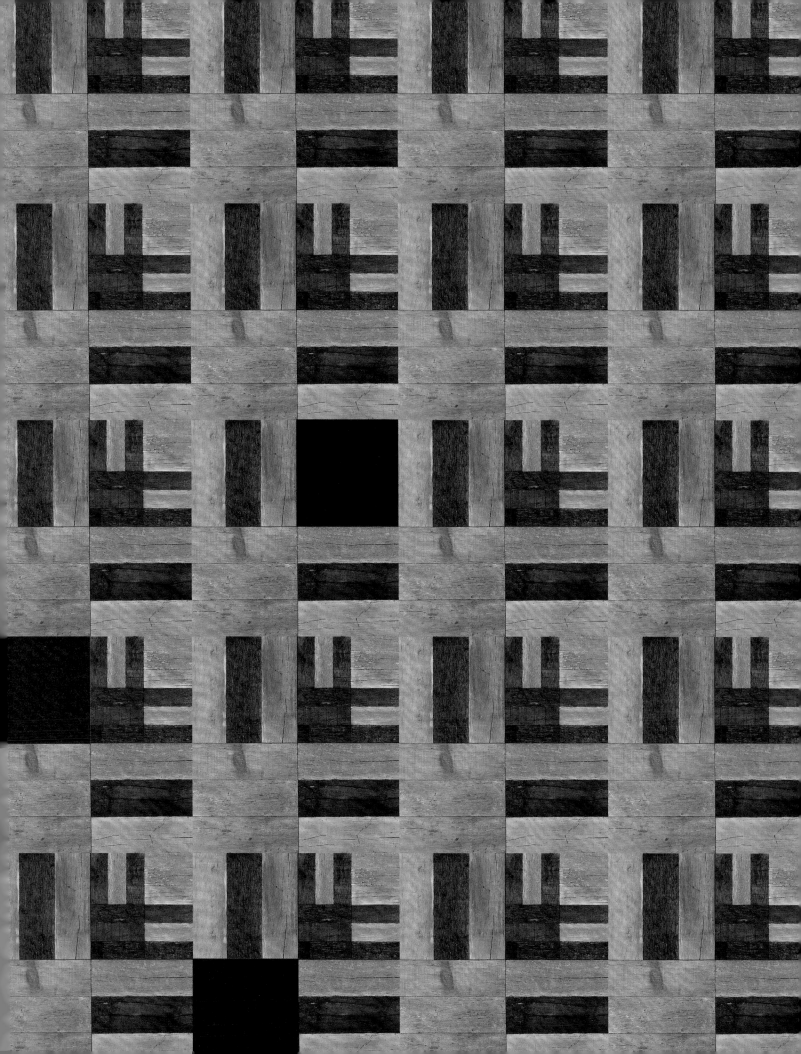

ANNIE LEIBOVITZ *A Photographer's Life* 1990–2005

When we got the phone call about this project, we worried that it would be a bit tricky because it wasn't about doing a whole house from scratch but about filling in holes in an already well-designed space. Both the architect and the original interior designer are people we respect and are, frankly, fans of. Our immediate thought was, how can Commune make this better? What is the missing layer?

After touring the house and immediately falling in love with our charismatic and lovely clients, we realized that they'd simply grown with time, but the house, meanwhile, had not changed with them. While the interiors were beautiful, they did not reflect their personalities or the casual, elegant, and effortless ways they entertain and live. With a new passion for art and two kids off to college (one remains at home), our clients were at a new and exciting stage in life. But the interiors were not a portrait of them as people or of their histories and collected heirlooms. Therein lies the narrative: This one was about real life.

With such good bones in place, we focused on layering in four design elements: color, texture, a playful scale, and what we at Commune call "smalls"—all the little objects and things you interact with that tell a story. These smalls are arguably the most important layer in a house.

In the living room, our priority was adding color and creating one large seating area rather than two separate areas. We had a black hemp-and-silk Commune Hex rug made to cover most of the room. The rug unifies the space and provides a mix of textures underfoot. The couch and the two armchairs were already in the house, but we changed the fill in the couch for added comfort, adjusted pillow sizes, and upholstered the couch in a mix of mohair jewel tones. The large Claro walnut coffee table was custom-made for the space by Alma Allen, then we layered in vintage side tables and leather-strap stools from Denmark. The plant in a David Cressey pot was brought in for scale. Having something that soft and tall extended the room into the space above and at the same time grounded the seating below, making it more casual and comfortable. The David Cressey thumbprint pots are incredible; they're art. In them you feel the artist's hand and can see the craft right away. For the more

it's what's on the inside that counts

personal layer, on the coffee table, newly painted blue bar, and bookshelves are a collection of art books, family heirlooms, and newly acquired smalls. Last, but not least, we hung the abstract painting by John McLaughlin above the fireplace; it was one of those serendipitous moments where everything came together around this painting.

In the dining room, we added color by upholstering the walls in a warm, oatmeal-colored wool, and the dining table was refinished in an indigo lacquer. The incredible chandelier was, again, a play on scale. It came from the Palace of the Republic in East Berlin. It's the "jewelry" in the room. The incredible Wolfgang Tillmans photograph anchors the room and pulls together all the colors.

For the study, our client wanted a room that had color and pattern and that felt more collected, slightly over the top, and more fun. From our shared love of Tony Duquette, came the brass Moroccan table, the coral, the beaded necklace, and the antique mirror panel above the fireplace. There's a polka dot, clamshell wallpaper on the ceiling. The desk behind the couch is a Rosewood Dutch modern piece. The fabric on the couch is an embroidered and hand-painted pattern on linen. The armchairs are Italian from the 1940s. Our client has incredible pottery and other pieces passed on to her from her designer mother.

The master bedroom needed warmth and color. We curated the shelves, which helped warm up the room. The vestibule to the master bedroom is painted a beautiful blue, and the wall behind the bed is almost black, yet these colors do not draw your attention. They flow seamlessly within a predominantly white space. We added texture with a black jute rug and beautifully made leather bedside tables by BDDW. The Italian linen curtains are also textured and have a large pattern. We re-covered the armchairs for added color and had a cashmere headboard, as well as a lot of bedding, custom-made for the room.

**photographs by lisa romerein
text by pamela shamshiri**

This beautiful house with incredible light needed its inhabitants to step forward and take over the space in a bolder, more lived-in way. It needed the personality, warmth, layers, and colors that come with living a rich and full life. In the end, we helped the interiors catch up to and reflect the lives of their inhabitants.

The dining room walls were re-covered in an oatmeal-colored wool for soundproofing, texture, and warmth. The chairs were part of our clients' collection. The artwork is by Wolfgang Tillmans. The chandelier is a module of a light fixture by Peter Rockel; this piece came out of the Palace of the Republic in East Berlin. The table runner is a giant kasuri waffle custom-made by Hiroko Takeda. The silver-rimmed bowl is by Masanobu Ando.

∨ For the study, our client wanted a Tony Duquette vibe—lots of color, pattern, and a quirky mix of pieces. We wallpapered the ceiling and changed the window treatments to matchstick roman blinds. The custom sofa is covered in a hand-painted and embroidered Manuel Canovas fabric. The ornate brass tray-top table is from the 1940s, and the armchairs are 1950s Italian. The artwork behind the desk is by Billy Al Bengston.

In the master bedroom, it became important to layer in texture and color. We painted the wall behind the bed Regent Green (almost black) by Benjamin Moore. The custom headboard is upholstered in Loro Piana cashmere; the coverlet fabric is by Rogers & Goffigon; and the blanket is mohair by Trove. The bedside sconces are by Serge Mouille. The vintage chairs are covered in a BDDW pink velvet.

A HOTEL ON THE CANAL

PHOTOGRAPHS BY SPENCER LOWELL · TEXT BY ROMAN ALONSO

When Alex Calderwood first told us about this project, my thinking was, "I'll go to Panama and check it out, but there's no way we are taking it on." Within hours of my arrival in Casco Antiguo, the oldest neighborhood in Panama City, I had decided otherwise. The place was a cross between Old Havana and New Orleans: Spanish Colonial architecture going back to the 1600s, touched by the French during their failed attempt to build the canal, was crumbling. The area had taken a downward turn during and after the Noriega years (mid- to late 1980s), and gangs had taken over. The old American Trade Building, future home of the American Trade Hotel, had been the headquarters for the most violent of the gangs. Covered in graffiti, the elevator shaft was filled with garbage five stories high. But things were starting to change, and Alex, with his amazing nose for the next best thing, had sniffed out the place and decided that an Ace hotel would put it on the map of cool.

The building had been purchased by locals who were thoughtfully and sustainably redeveloping the Casco neighborhood into a more appealing alternative to the booming, glittering mass of hotels and casinos across the bay. The site of the future hotel was made up of four buildings ranging in style from Art Deco to French Colonial, the main building being an undecipherable opulent mash-up of styles. There was a beautiful courtyard and a rooftop with 360-degree views. The bones were too good to pass up. Alex said he wanted it to be like one of those hotels in a Humphrey Bogart movie, filled with writers and spies; he wanted it to feel like something that had always been there.

We came up with a narrative that involved a family of hoteliers who had built the hotel back in the canal boom years in the nineteen teens and had always run it as if it was their home, each generation bringing with them the style of their time and their finds from travels around the globe. We wanted the spaces to feel collected, residential, and safe—a refuge from the grittiness of the neighborhood. And since this would be a sister hotel in the Ace family of hotels, and outside the brand's highly democratic and urban aesthetic, we could experiment and invent a new type of luxury that played into all the things Ace and Commune mutually love: the local, the handcrafted, the honest, the real.

We looked at furniture designed by Clara Porset in Mexico in the 1960s and made our designs in Nicaragua of the most beautiful local wood that had washed ashore during hurricanes. Every piece is hardwood; not a single sheet of veneer was used on the project. We searched all over for antiques in the colonial and hacienda styles. All light fixtures are custom, inspired by the work of Mathieu Matégot, the Austrian secessionist style, and Italian design from the 1970s and 1980s. All sofas are English, by George Smith, upholstered in tropical prints. Back in Los Angeles, Michael Boyd made some beautiful chairs lacquered in a Le Corbusier green, and Tanya Aguiñiga made a series of wall hangings out of cotton rope, "nine sisters" that hang in the dining room. In Texas, James Garza made iron and leather hacienda-style furniture for the guest rooms and courtyard. We enlisted local artist Ana Elena Garuz to paint a mural in the lobby area, an abstract aerial interpretation of the Panama Canal. And most importantly, there had to be plants everywhere. We worked with Matthew Brown, our favorite landscape designer, who put together a collection of indigenous plants handpicked from nurseries he tracked down all over Panama. An indoor jungle was the inspiration.

The spaces are light and tropical and elegant, and they speak of a place that's always been at a cultural crossroads, filled with foreign correspondents and spies and intrigue, just like Alex wanted.

< The façade of the American Trade Hotel in Casco Antiguo, Panama. The building dates from 1917.

The lobby area is lined with custom cement tile made in Costa Rica. All millwork was designed by the architecture team Hache Uve and built on site of local woods.

The brass lighting fixtures, inspired by Joseph Hoffman's designs for the Sanatorium Purkersdorf outside Vienna, were made in Los Angeles by Atelier de Troupe.

The custom concrete pots were made locally from mid-century modern designs. The landscape design is by Matthew Brown. The Thonet rockers have seats upholstered in denim, and in the café, white Bertoia chairs were upholstered with bone-color ultra suede.

> The furniture in the lobby was inspired by designs by Clara Porset and fabricated from local hardwoods in Nicaragua. The webbing on the chairs is nylon. The chairs lined up against the wall are nineteenth-century colonial antiques.

‹ The rectory table was custom-made in Nicaragua. The armchairs
   are Mission-style antiques from Mexico. The lacquered chairs in
   Le Corbusier green are PLANEfurniture by Michael Boyd.

The sofa is by George Smith, the coffee table is custom-made in
Nicaragua, and the club chairs are by James Garza from Marfa, Texas.

In the restaurant, the tables were custom-made, with zinc tops and carved wood bases. The chairs are our design, made in Nicaragua with saddle leather seats and jute backs. The light fixtures are our design, made by Atelier de Troupe. The wall hangings are of cotton rope by Mexican-American artist Tanya Aguiñiga.

A view of the pool and Casco Viejo from the courtyard balconies.

The powder-coated, perforated light fixtures on the railings are by Atelier de Troupe from our design.

> In the courtyard, powder-coated metal furniture is by Atelier de Troupe with Knoll Bertoia dining chairs and leather-and-metal lounge chairs by James Garza.

A George Smith sofa in the library sits side by side with furniture inspired by Clara Porset.

> In the guest rooms the floors are made from salvaged local hardwood. All wood furniture is custom-made in Nicaragua. The dining chairs are by James Garza.

The decorative pillows were embroidered by artisans in Chiapas, Mexico, and the hand-loomed, Mossi textile blankets are by dosa.

> A bathroom with a view of the canal. Bathroom fixtures by Waterworks and custom floor tile made in Costa Rica.

LIKE A TREEHOUSE

I will never forget my husband's gasp when we first saw the Lechner House. It was loud and clear: He had fallen in love with the house the instant the gate opened and revealed the long, diagonal of the living-room window. For myself, I was gasping at the deplorable condition of the house and the nearly unrecognizable 1948 Schindler interior. It required a full revitalization. It would be too much work for us and more importantly, for Commune, at the time. But eventually I would change my mind.

Nonetheless, when you entered, you felt suspended in space. To this day, you feel you are floating above the hills. Below the windows of the great room is the bowl of the canyon and spread out before you are trees, just treetops in every direction. The house follows the grade line perfectly. It's nestled in the V of the canyon, and the house itself is a wide V-plan with two axes angling off. The hearth in the great room is placed at the point of the "V" plan. This affords the longest views, layered with glass, wood, and light in every direction. To paraphrase Esther McCoy, Schindler let the land dictate the house rather than letting the house impose on the land. The feeling is one of standing on a suspended platform covered by a tent. The roof soars and floats above the living room. The structure is paper thin, light, and indeed tent-like.

The great room is one of the best and last still-standing examples of Schindler's more expressionistic and raw "space architecture" from the late 1940s. It is a spatial cave for viewing nature. You sit at a brick hearth, with the more solid side of the house behind you. The space opens up much like a cave does. Before designing this house, Schindler had traveled to the Anasazi cave dwellings in the Southwest and on the same trip visited several pueblos. As early as 1912, Schindler wrote in his manifesto: "The cave was the original dwelling. The hollow adobe pile was the first permanent house ... The technique of architect and sculptor were similar ... The architect has finally discovered the medium of his art: SPACE." Schindler sculpted space. Space was always his overarching focus. Everything he did was in support of the space; everything else, he simplified.

PHOTOGRAPHS BY FRANÇOIS HALARD   TEXT BY PAMELA SHAMSHIRI

< This is the view of the great room, looking from the hearth toward the trees. The original dining table is to the left with dining chairs Schindler designed for the house. We reconstructed them based on some sketches and photographs we found and upholstered them in raw silk. The table pulls out of the wall to seat six. There are two planters just outside the great room window.

> This is the view of the great room, looking from the kitchen toward the dining room, which is placed just beyond the slatted wood walls. The quintessential Schindler fireplace is made of stainless steel. The hearth is located at the point of the "V-shaped" ground plan. There are planters in the brick columns and a trellis above the fireplace. The angled couches are designed by Schindler and recovered in mohair. We have a collection of 1920s Khotan rugs that we roll up and move out depending on what is happening in the room. The Schindler-designed tea carts are made of glass and wood and have Plexiglas wheels.

This is my son, Basel, and me in the great room. You can see the soaring roofline, system of beams, datum lines, clerestories, and the "shoji ladders" outside that hold up the overhang of both the great room and the dining room.

The dining room was originally an outdoor patio that Schindler later enclosed. The dining table and chairs by Piet Hein Eek were bought on a whim in Amsterdam. In spirit, Hein Eek's designs are akin to Schindler's. The overhead light is a Noguchi and the rug is by Commune. The geometric pattern came from a painting that Steven Johanknecht, of Commune, did in college.

With the support of an excellent team at Commune, we embarked on a two-year excavation, restoration, and renovation project. We restored every window and surface of the original part of the house and paid homage with a fresh eye to the additions of the house. Underneath all the drywall, granite, terra-cotta tile, metal windows, block glass, and paint were the original construction-grade wood panels, with Schindler's numbers scribbled everywhere, along with notes on colors, ideas for windows, and even a quintessential stainless steel fireplace. The wood panels have no value. They're construction-grade plywood with a "color wash" on them. There's no hardware. The windows could not be simpler. Most are fixed, some are awning, and some slide open to catch the hilltop wind. We had the original set of drawings, and we also had a ton of beautiful photos, and the two rarely matched. These, along with the excavation, gave us insight into Schindler's mind and an education on his process. There were no dimensions or notes on the windows, because he just changed them on the job. As he figured out the light and sculpted the space, he made adjustments to the design on the spot. He embraced the process of both the construction and the design. He was spontaneous and flexible within the discipline of a controlling idea about space. He simplified everything else.

Schindler is perhaps the least understood and most underappreciated of the American pioneers of modern architecture. And yet he is an architect's architect and perhaps the most borrowed. Schindler sought to transform low art into high art through the poetic use of standard everyday materials. This house remains as a remarkable example of the union of the two. With this spirit and notion in mind, we started designing very purposeful, custom pieces of furniture and millwork to fulfill various needs. By engaging in this process, we gained both a sense of freedom and a very specific problem-solving approach. That is perhaps our biggest take-away at Commune, that you can play the low card and the high card at the same time—that is, an ace. What's important is how you design it.

At Commune, we always embrace the sense of the person, of the human touch. Schindler was masterful at this and took us to the next level. His houses are intimate portraitures. He had a deep insight into human nuances, and they are reflected in his designs, particularly the built-ins. For instance, there is a perfect drink rail at the edge of the great room sofas. They angle out to such a perfect position that one would never place a drink anywhere else. If you want to have a more formal conversation, you sit at the shallow end of the angled couches and pull the wheeled tea cart around. If you want to lie down and read, there is the deep end of the couch, with ledges and reading cubbies nearby. The original dining table pulls out of the wall and extends into the room when needed. There is a perfect place to make a drink. Somehow, you can't bring yourself to place any furniture in front of the great room window. It blocks the view. While the room supports a number of activities and is quite transformative, at its core it's a spatial cave for viewing nature. Every interior design decision has to support that or it simply doesn't work.

We've experimented and learned a lot, as far as color and contrasts. If Schindler were here he'd say, "No contrast, no acid, no pastels, no sheen!" It's all shading with nature and very few colors. It's the gray tones of the rocks and the yellow-brown leaves of Southern California. In Schindler's words, "A California house will have to join the basic color character of its setting." This means natural colors, natural materials, nubby textures, low contrast, monochromatic shading. It's cubism, expressionism—not de Stijl. Unknowingly, we had signed up to restore something that is at the heart of what Commune is about: simplicity, intimacy, lack of ostentation, equality, process, the mixing of high and low, the exercise of frugality, maximization, geometry, a no-waste approach, respecting the architecture with the furnishings. It's not self-conscious, not scholarly; there is a love of the site and nature, a love of California, and it's raw and refined all at the same time. It holds the lessons we needed to experience firsthand.

So now my family lives in a house that is not meant to be furnished, but the trade-off is, we live in a sculpture. It's a vehicle for a life that is filled with movement, rhythm, light, and poetry: It's ever changing and always in motion, much like we are. Today, this quirky spaceship of a house anticipates the future as much as it did in 1948.

The kitchen is completely new and designed in the style of Schindler. We removed a bathroom to make this long, thirty-foot galley kitchen that opens up to the family room. The handles and notches are a combination of ones that Schindler used throughout the 1940s. The awning-style windows are not original, but there was a version of them in a kitchen elevation that was never built. The small ledges, spice cubbies, and open shelving are all borrowed details from several different kitchens.

The family room was originally a grassed outdoor terrace, but it was enclosed in the 1980s. To tie it to the rest of the house, we incorporated the datum line into the design of the cedar walls and bookshelves throughout. The wood box with the brass doors hides the television. The wool rug is from the Atlas Mountains in Morocco. The coffee table is by Alma Allen; the rock base was cast from an actual rock. John Williams designed the kids' desks. The wall color is a custom mix by Commune, based on Heath Ceramics clay.

The kids' room is painted gray and has two sets of Ikea bunks in it. We bought a third set of bunks and reconfigured it to create bookshelves above their heads and toy storage on the upper level.

The gym was originally an outdoor patio that was enclosed in the 1980s as well. It's the most used and popular room in the house. The basketball hoop was a gift from John Williams. The walls are Homasote for hanging art and banging into. The yellow curtain is made of burlap; it's excellent as a backdrop for performances.

The laundry room is made up of a series of pegboard closets that wrap around the entire room. It holds not only linens and a vintage fabric collection but also the television and music components, a vase closet, a gift closet, all the home supplies, and so on. The metal rail around the room is great for drying clothes. The countertop is Masonite with a stainless edge. My favorite feature is the larger closet at the back accessed by a sliding door. When the closet light is on, the pegboard is back lit and light streams through the holes.

The master bedroom is downstairs in what was once Dr. Lechner's office. The brass and walnut bed is by Alma Allen. The bedcover and pouf are by dosa. The bookshelves are custom.

WE THANK OUR LUCKY STARS AND...

OUR STAFF PAST AND PRESENT FOR THEIR HARD WORK, GREAT TALENT AND DEDICATION. THE ARTISTS, ARTISANS AND CRAFTS-MEN – OUR EXTENDED FAMILY - FOR BRINGING BEAUTY AND SOUL INTO OUR PROJECTS. THE CLIENTS FOR THEIR TRUST, THE END-LESS VARIETY OF PROJECTS AND FOR THE LESSONS LEARNED. OUR DEALERS, VENDORS, BUILDERS AND MANUFACTURERS - THERE WOULD BE NOTHING TO SHOW IN THIS BOOK WITHOUT YOU. THE PHOTOGRAPHERS AND CONTRIBUTORS FEATURED AND OUR WON-DERFUL EDITOR - PERCEPTION IS REALITY - WITH THIS BOOK YOU'VE HELPED US MAKE IT A BEAUTIFUL ONE. OUR FRIENDS AND FAMILY FOR THEIR LOVE AND LIMITLESS PATIENCE. AND TO THOSE OF YOU WHO HAVE FOLLOWED AND SUPPORTED OUR WORK FOR THE PAST DECADE...HOPE YOU ENJOY THE BOOK, IT'S DEDICATED TO YOU.

Edited by Andrea Danese
Designed by Commune and Lorraine Wild
Production by True Sims

Library of Congress Control Number: 2014930549

ISBN: 978-1-4197-0963-0

Printed and bound in China
10 9 8 7 6 5

Abrams books are available at special discounts when purchased in quantity for premiums and promotions as well as
fundraising or educational use. Special editions can also be
created to specification. For details, contact specialsales@
abramsbooks.com or the address below.

ABRAMS The Art of Books
195 Broadway, New York, NY 10007
abramsbooks.com